SIT WITHIN, AND YOU WILL FIND INFINITY WAITING

DISCOVER

The Universe in You

AKSHATA V NOOLI

BlueRose ONE
Stories Matter
NewDelhi • London

BLUEROSE PUBLISHERS
India | U.K.

For permissions requests or inquiries regarding this publication, please contact:

BLUEROSE PUBLISHERS
www.BlueRoseONE.com
info@bluerosepublishers.com
+91 8882 898 898
+4407342408967

ISBN: 978-93-7310-169-9

Cover design: Daksh
Typesetting: Tanya Raj Upadhyay

First Edition: December 2025

To my baby, Vivikta, for making me feel so special about life, parents Sri Vasant Ramachandra Nooli and Smt Nanda Vasant Nooli who have been a prime support, of course, they are the source of my energy, loving siblings and wonderful husband, who cheered me while he was alive and continues to teach me the greatest life lessons even after he has left the world. It's through these experiences that I have discovered the universe within myself!

A Note from Akshata

If you've picked up this book, something in you is already reaching for more clarity, more peace, more of *you*.

If you picked up this book, something in you is already reaching for more clarity, more peace, even after we have left the world. It's through these experiences that I have discovered the quiet, transformative spaces of coaching, healing, and handwriting analysis. Along the way, I've learned that the answers we seek rarely live "out there". They've been quietly waiting within us all along.

This book is my way of holding up a mirror so you can see the constellations inside you — the strengths, the stories, the light you may have forgotten. Take what resonates, leave what doesn't, and above all, be gentle with yourself as you turn these pages.

This book is my way of holding up a mirror.

—Akshata V Nooli

Preface:

"A person is healthy—when he is both physically and mentally fit. But when you adapt this art, you'll attain your higher spiritual self, and that is when you'll be called perfectly healthy."

Health is alignment of the physical, mental and spiritual Self. This book gives an insight into how to gel magically with today's world, overcoming our insecurities, fear and doubtfulness with better understanding of our mighty Universe—as all the answers to our challenges are hidden within us when we learn this beautiful connection.

Why should I read this book?

This book is crafted purely out of love and care to build the connection between the outer world and the inner self. As you go through the book, you'll experience that you don't just go with words, rather, the blanks demand and tingle you to fill them up; it seeks for your opinions. I promise, as you move along with the book, you'll fall in love with yourself. And that's my purpose too! To introduce your power-self to you!

This book provides insights on how to become the best version of yourself. So, without further delay, fasten your seatbelts and prepare for an incredible journey into your inner self with me.

Table of Contents

Chapter 1
Universe

What is the Universe?

The essence of our existence:

Everything in the universe is ultimately composed of one fundamental element: "Matter."

During a lecture, my physics professor walked around the room and explained the concept of the Universe. Using everyday objects as analogies, she described how everything in the universe is composed of cells. The word "UNIVERSE" is derived from two words: "Uni" and "Verse." "Uni" means one, representing the totality, the entirety, the summary. "Verse" refers to rhythm. Understanding the entire life form, the totality in rhythm, is what comprises our UNIVERSE.

Isn't that wonderful?

Matter is a substance that possesses mass and occupies space. It can exist in various forms such as solid, liquid, gas, or plasma. In the realm of science, we acknowledge that everything is composed of matter, and it cannot be created or destroyed. Similarly, in our holy book "Bhagwat Geeta," there are references that state our soul is eternal, undergoing a cycle of shedding old bodies and acquiring new ones, much like changing clothes.

Given that we are all composed of the same substance, matter, what distinguishes us from other creatures?

It is the power of our thoughts!

Now, what is the power of thoughts?

Thoughts possess incredible power. As human beings, we have the remarkable ability to think, allowing us to create and shape our own thoughts. Hold on to this word, “thought”; let me amaze you with an interesting fact: what if I told you that it is your thought that is responsible for the fever, cold, anger, happiness? I am not kidding you, a single thought is responsible even for the cancerous cells to take birth in your body. Having said that, if we are ignorant, we will keep thinking negative about ourselves and wish bad things on others too. But the best part is, we can use this as a boon. Didn’t you get me???

You can change the world with your invisible power of thoughts. You can cure diseases too.

In physics, the speed of light in air is approximately 299,705 kilometers per second, while the speed of sound in air is about 343 meters per second.

However, it's fascinating to realize that our thoughts travel virtually instantaneously. When we think of a friend, they receive the message in less than a second. In fact, our thoughts move even faster than the speed of light, which is approximately 300,000,000 meters per second.

Let’s jump into the next most important and inevitable source which enables us to stay alive on earth.

While thinking of this, a small yet powerful incident I am reminded off, and that I can’t resist to share with you all.

Once, when Swami Vivekananda asked if he had seen God, Ramakrishna Paramhamsa responded, "Yes, I see God as I see you."

Through dedicated practice and wisdom, we ultimately discover the truth of oneness. "Aham Brahmasmi" (we all possess the supreme energy within us, in the form of oxygen) holds true. This is why it is referred to as "Prana-Vayu" (where "Prana" represents life, and "Vayu" signifies air).

Our bodies are composed of the panch-tattva or the "pancha bhutas," which are the fundamental five elements: Prithvi (Earth), Jal (Water), Agni (Fire), Vayu (Air), and Akash (Ether) (Space).

72% of our body consists of water, 12% of earth, 6% of air, 4% of fire, and 6% is attributed to space.

These four elements serve as the foundation of our creation, crucial for living a fulfilling life. The fifth element, space, extends beyond the physical realm and encompasses mystical dimensions.

Our bodies are a manifestation of the interplay between these five elements, just like the world and the universe. In the yogic system, our bodies are believed to have 72,000 nadis (energy channels) converging at 114 junctions known as chakras. Among these chakras, 112 are located inside the body, while 2 are positioned outside. Out of the 112 chakras, 4 chakras naturally align themselves without any effort. The remaining 108 chakras require attention and effort to bring them into balance.

To address these 108 chakras, Eastern practices often involve performing activities 108 times. For instance, you may have observed people chanting mantras with a strand of 108 beads. This connection to the number 108 reflects the harmony between our individual selves and the vast universe. From a scientific standpoint, this correlation can be understood as follows:

The sun's diameter surpasses the distance between the earth and the sun by a factor of 108, while the moon's diameter is 108 times smaller than the distance between the earth and the moon. Moreover, the diameters of the moon and the sun also maintain a 108:1 ratio.

Our bodies contain a network of 108 chakras/nadis that offer avenues for exploration and improvement. This cosmic alignment intricately connects us with the universe, highlighting the profound interrelation between the external and internal. It powerfully conveys the concept, "The Universe is within You!!!" By harmonizing the five elements (panch tattvas) within ourselves, we tap into exceptional capabilities waiting to be unleashed.

The wonders occurring within us far surpass what we observe in the external world.

A single thought has a power to create or destroy the world which is our intangible asset. The panch tattvas being our tangible asset.

Can you imagine when we analyze these two treasures and make the best use of it ....????

Anything which you can think of becomes achievable, when alignment is just right.

With that we shall dive into the most vital topic.

Our Body – Our Health.

Chapter 2
Health and Stability

Maintaining strong mental, physical, and emotional health is essential for attaining success. Neglecting self-care in these areas can impede progress in other aspects of life. Therefore, it is vital to prioritize the well-being of your mind, body, and relationships to thrive and achieve your goals.

By dedicating time to self-care and nurturing these three pillars, you can reap substantial rewards in the long run. Regard your body as a temple, and place a high priority on health and stability in your daily life. True well-being encompasses physical, mental, emotional, and spiritual aspects, and achieving this requires finding a harmonious balance in our diet, exercise routines, restful sleep, effective stress management strategies, and lifestyle habits.

By prioritizing the consumption of nutritious whole foods over empty calories that offer little nutritional value, we lay the groundwork for optimal functioning of all body systems. Incorporating regular exercise into our routine helps prevent potential illnesses, as it keeps muscles toned, strengthens organs, and regulates weight levels. Moreover, exercise triggers the release of endorphins, contributing to maintaining positive moods.

Making time for daily relaxation can be incredibly beneficial, especially when facing challenging emotions or situations. Deep breathing exercises are a proven way to calm a stressed mind, offering immediate relief and long-term advantages. Embracing these practices allows for valuable moments of tranquility in our lives.

By consciously making daily efforts to break negative life patterns, like excessive smoking or drinking, we can significantly enhance our overall vitality. Additionally, taking steps to reduce environmental pollution simultaneously brings considerable benefits not only to our personal health but also to the broader goal of achieving planetary sustainability.

As you recognize the sacredness within yourself, it becomes evident that nurturing a loving and caring approach from within is the path to success. By prioritizing the cultivation of inner strength through nurturing practices, you can experience profound self-appreciation, akin to the way every temple is blessed anew by the divine.

Chakras

"Chakra" is a Sanskrit term that means "Wheel." There are seven chakras, these spinning centers located within the core of our body. These chakras act as conduits for universal energy, aligning along the spine and connecting our mind, physical body, and spiritual essence. Through meditation, we can transcend the limitations of the physical dimension. On the other hand, yoga helps us understand and align our system with the cosmic geometry.

The energy, frequency, and functions of each chakra are directly linked to its corresponding color, body organs, levels of consciousness, and natural elements. These connections are firmly grounded in science. When the mind, body, and soul are in perfect alignment, the chakras are balanced, leading to harmony in our Yin-Yang energy.

Chakra	Element	Location	Gland	Sound	Frequency (in Hz)	Problems Faced due to blockages	Functions
Crown Chakra SAHASRARA	None	Crown of the Head	Hypothalamus and pituitary	OM	963	Loneliness, Depression	Understand
Third Eye Chakra AJNA	Light	Between eye-brows	Pineal	OM	852	Nightmare, poor eye-sight	See
Throat Chakra VISHUDDHA	Space	Base of Throat	Jaw, teeth, throat	HAM	741	Can't express, Lack of confidence	Talk
Heart Chakra ANAHATA	Air	Centre of chest	Thymus and Lymph	YAM	639	Feeling Unloved, Heart broken	Love
Solar Plexus Chakra MANIPURA	Fire	Above the navel,	Digestive system and adrenal Glands	RAM	528	Angry, Helpless	Determination
Sacral Chakra SVADHISHTHANA	Water	Lower Abdomen	Reproductive organs	VAM	417	Poor Intuition	Feel
Root Chakra MULADHARA	Earth	Base of the spine	Gonads	LAM	369	Low Self esteem	I am

The Seven Chakras represents seven different colours as in rainbow,

Crown Chakra-Violet or White

Third Eye Chakra- Indigo

Throat Chakra- Blue

Heart Chakra- Green

Solar Plexus Chakra- Yellow

Sacral Chakra- Orange

Root Chakra- Red

Understanding the essence of each Chakra, including the sound it enhances, its frequency, the glands it affects, and the colour it represents, practicing yoga becomes an excellent method to balance the elements in our body. This alignment will result in physical, mental, and emotional calmness.

"A person is healthy –When he is both physically and mentally fit

but when you adapt this art you'll attain your higher spiritual self

and that is when you'll be called perfectly healthy"

Health is Alignment of physical, Mental and Spiritual Self

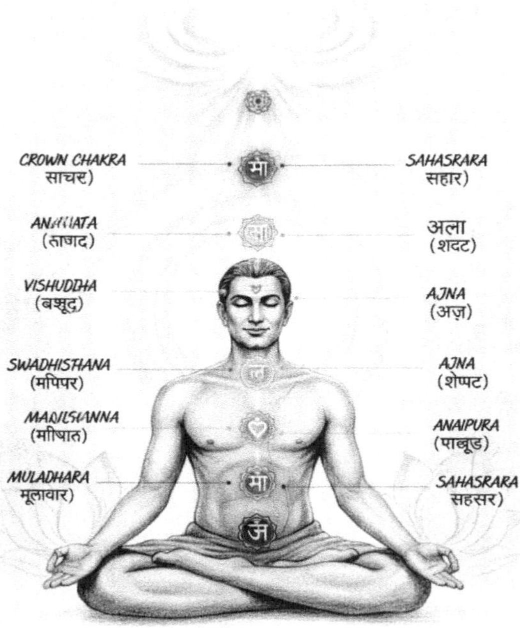
CROWN CHAKRA
साचर)
SAHASRARA
सहार)
अला
(शदट)
VISHUDDHA
(बश्रूद)
AJNA
(अज़)
SWADHISTHANA
(मपिपर)
AJNA
(शेप्पट)
(मीषात)
ANAIPURA
(पाब्रूड)
MULADHARA
मूलावार)
SAHASRARA
सहसर)

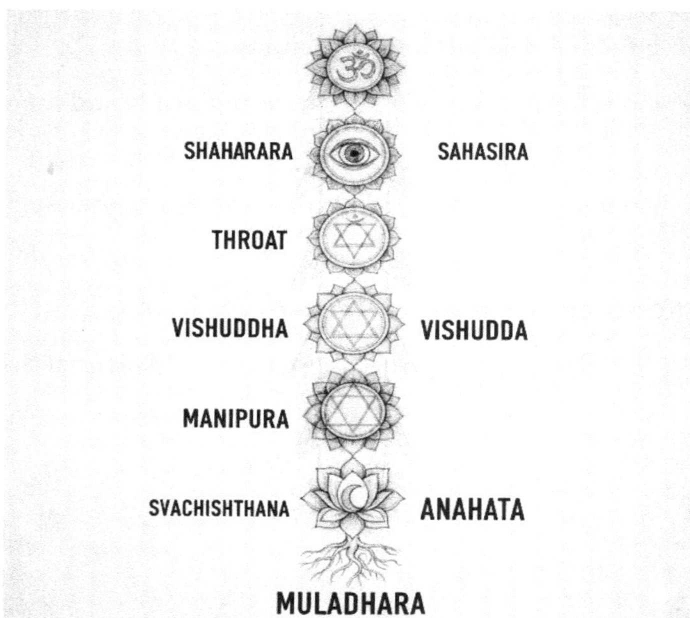
SHAHARARA
SAHASIRA
THROAT
VISHUDDHA
VISHUDDA
MANIPURA
SVACHISHTHANA
ANAHATA
MULADHARA

Chapter 3
Gratitude

"Cultivate the habit of being grateful for every good thing that comes to you, and to give thanks continuously. And because all things have contributed to your advancement, you should include all things in your gratitude."

Ralph Waldo Emerson

The term "Gratitude" has its roots in the Latin word "gratus," which translates to being thankful. In simpler terms, it is a way of expressing appreciation for the kindness or gifts we receive from others.

"Thank you" is one of the most frequently used phrases, whether it's people wishing us on special occasions or offering well wishes for exams. It comes naturally as a reflex when a small favor is done. Practicing gratitude helps us cultivate stronger relationships. When we sincerely feel and express gratitude and appreciation to the people in our lives, it creates bonds of love, builds trust, and brings us closer together.

Researchers have found that practicing gratitude and expressing appreciation can have a substantial positive impact on our mental health. However, when it comes to our connection with the divine and the universe, we often overlook or underestimate its significance. We rarely make time or consider it important to express gratitude for the remarkable things happening around us. Instead, we often focus on asking for more, rather than being grateful for the blessings we already have. Nevertheless, the universe doesn't function in a way where constant asking leads to lasting fulfillment, even if all our desires were to be fulfilled.

"Universe has everything

we just need to "ask" our wishes will be fulfilled,

-on the contrary

Universe doesn't fulfill our dreams if we just ask for"

Let's gain a clear understanding of this concept:

It is an undeniable truth that no desire is too immense for the universe to fulfill. As we learned in the previous chapter, whether we perceive ourselves as individuals or the universe itself, we are fundamentally interconnected. At the energy level, we are all united as one.

Yes, there is a method to ask the universe for anything, and it follows a specific pattern!

Excited to learn?

Let me share a small example:

When I was in 3rd grade, my elder sister and brother were in 6th and 9th grade respectively. Our father had been away in Delhi for work for three long months. Before his return, we were given the chance to write a letter to him, expressing anything we wanted or desired. Despite the existence of landline phones, we preferred writing letters and sending them via speed post for more meaningful communication. Throughout my life, being the youngest, I have always been cherished and loved.

Each of us contributed two lines to the same letter. My brother wrote, "Dear Papa, we all miss you. I'm studying diligently, but I need to prepare for my preparatory exams. Thank you for the science book you sent last month; it's been incredibly helpful. As I don't have a maths refresher, I borrowed one from my seniors. I'm taking care of my sisters and listening to Amma. Please come home soon."

My sister wrote, "Papa, I am attending school regularly. The teacher appreciated my singing and suggested to practise classical music as I have potential. I won the 1st prize in calligraphy, which they announced during the morning assembly. Love you, Papa."

Then it was my turn - I wrote, "Dear Papa, I am feeling upset because it's been three months since you've been away from us. I lost my magic Kapali pencil, and I wish to have a replacement. I also have a desire to own a piano like my friend because I admire it, and some chocolates would be lovely too. In your last letter, there was no mention of me, and it made me feel sad. Love you, Papa."

After a few days, my father returned, and as expected, he brought gifts for all of us. My brother received his maths refresher and some pocket money for the picnic. My sister got a "Hero" pen, which improved her handwriting (it was a popular ink pen back in the 90s), and she also received a piano, leading us both to start attending music classes. As for me, I received two large Cadbury chocolates, but I was still not content despite the generous gift. We all thanked Papa for the beautiful presents, but my dissatisfaction lingered.

Yes, I understand that many of you can relate to a similar situation at home. Let's break it down into smaller parts to learn and understand more effectively. In the story, I used my father as an example, but now you can take "father" to represent the universe, the almighty, your boss at the office, your institution, or anyone else—it applies universally.

Now, let's analyze what we can learn from this story. Firstly, when we express gratitude, we demonstrate to the higher powers that we appreciate their presence in our lives, resulting in attracting more positive things. My brother expressed gratitude for the science book, and without explicitly asking for it, he received the maths refresher. Similarly, my sister received the pen and piano as a result of her efforts in calligraphy and singing; she didn't explicitly ask for them. In contrast, I only received two chocolates because I focused more on complaining rather than expressing gratitude. Moreover, when I asked for chocolates, I didn't specify the quantity, so receiving two seemed like a considerable number to me.

We should nurture gratitude for what we have because there is no living being in the world who has nothing to be thankful to the almighty for. Even on the days when we feel distressed, unimportant, or worthless, if we observe closely, we will find numerous reasons to be grateful. The fresh air we breathe, the clean water we drink, the rhythmic beating of our hearts, and the shelter we have over our heads are just a few examples. There are infinite reasons to find happiness; the key is to focus on the positive aspects and amplify them tenfold. By doing so, the universe itself will be compelled to provide us with abundant blessings. Instead of asking, it is better to feel a sense of obligation and praise the almighty for generously providing us with everything we need. Alongside that, we should work towards achieving our goals and desires. At some point in our lives, all of us have engaged in complaining about our circumstances.

Activity:

Here is an activity on gratitude. Take a moment to create a list of 21 things in your life that you are grateful for. You can express gratitude for anything and everything you appreciate. Make it a daily practice for 21 days. (The duration of 21 days is considered effective in establishing a habit by repeating it until it becomes ingrained in our subconscious mind.)

If you find it challenging to identify something to be grateful for or feel unsure about what to express gratitude towards, I will now offer you a list of 15 things to consider...

- Thank you, universe, for the peaceful sleep and the joy of waking up each morning.
- Thank you so much, universe, for blessing me with excellent health.
- Thank you, universe, for the gift of breathing fresh air and the happiness it brings.
- Thank you, universe, for providing me with a home to live in.
- Thank you, universe, for granting me a wonderful family. I feel incredibly lucky to have my parents, who are a constant source of energy for me.
- Thank you so much for my siblings, who always support me in all my endeavors.
- Thank you for the fan/AC in my room, and thank you to the table that assists me in my writing.
- Thank you for my phone, laptop, and internet connection.
- Thank you for the privilege of owning my own car/vehicle.
- Thank you, universe, for blessing me with an understanding and caring partner.
- Thank you, universe, for the gift of having two wonderful kids in my life.
- Thank you for the essential appliances such as the fridge, mixer, cooker, and the plates.
- Thank you, universe, for the career path I am currently pursuing.
- Thank you, universe, for the financial resources I have.
- Thank you, universe, for everything that is unfolding in my life.

My gratitude list:

1. ______________________________

2. ______________________________

3. ______________________________

4. ______________________________

5. ______________________________

6. ______________________________

7. ______________________________

8. ______________________________

9. ______________________________

10. ____

11. ____

12. ____

13. ____

14. ____

15. ____

16. ____

17. ____

18. ____

19. ____

20. ____

21. ____

Now that we understand how and what to express gratitude for, it's time to share a secret with you. And that secret is that we should be grateful for both the blessings we have and the challenging or difficult times we face.

Yes, you read it correctly. We should express gratitude even for the hardships.

As human beings, we often resist change, especially when it involves aspects such as illness, job loss, breakups, or the loss of loved ones. We feel hurt and find it challenging to accept these harsh realities. However, based on my personal experience, I can tell you that acceptance is the key to eventually overcoming these challenges.

The moment we embrace our situations and circumstances as they are, you can witness the magic unfolding—the magic being courage.

"Courage is that magical power

which is inbuilt in each one of us,

it sprouts within you

only when your acceptance mode is on"

Let me share a fascinating story to help you understand this better:

Once upon a time, in the early days of Gautam Buddha, he was walking through a dense forest when a group of monkeys started following him. Buddha tried to walk faster, but the monkeys kept up and made a lot of noise. A passer-by who had been living in the forest for many years noticed Buddha and offered some advice, "They are just monkeys, and as a human, you are stronger than any creature in the universe. Stop and face the monkeys, look into their eyes directly, and they will run away." Young Gautam followed this advice, and to his surprise, the monkeys quickly got scared and vanished from sight.

The lesson here is that if we keep running away from our problems, they will keep chasing us. However, when we gather the courage to confront them directly, the problems often disappear. "Acceptance is the key." Additionally, we can express gratitude by saying, "Thank you, God, for the challenges in my life. I am learning so much from them. Thank you for making me stronger."

Understanding is the first step to acceptance,

and only with acceptance can there be recovery

– J.K. Rowling

As we conclude our discussion on gratitude, let's now shift our focus to a universal healing technique. This method not only helps in healing oneself but also aids in gaining clarity of thoughts. Let's explore it further in detail.

I AM SORRY
PLEASE FORGIVE ME
I LOVE YOU
THANK YOU
THE POWER OF MAGICAL WORDS

Chapter 4
Universal healing ho'oponopono

To gain a deeper understanding of this unique method, we should explore its history, the true meaning of the word, why it is known as a Hawaiian method, how it became so popular, and its significance. Let's dive deep into it and uncover more!

Dr IHALEAKALA HEW LEN

Birth- April 1939 Death – Jan 15, 2022

Hawaii is a group of volcanic islands located in the central Pacific Ocean. These islands are situated 2,397 miles (3,857 km) east of San Francisco, California, and 5,293 miles (8,516 km) west of Manila, Philippines. The healing process we are discussing is commonly known as the Hawaiian method, as it was first discovered here by a clinical psychologist.

Dr. Ihaleakala Hew Len, born in April 1939, was raised on the Leeward Coast of Oahu and received his education at Kamehameha Schools in Hawaii. As a clinical psychologist, he encountered a remarkable challenge when he had to treat patients who were not only mentally ill but also displayed violent and harmful behavior towards themselves and others. These patients were so dangerous that their hands and legs were restrained with iron cuffs to prevent physical harm. The situation was truly alarming, and even hospital caregivers were afraid to interact with them or provide them with basic necessities like food and water.

However, what's truly astonishing is that Dr. Hew Len treated all of these patients without even seeing them in person. In fact, some reports suggest that he never set foot inside the hospital. The staff, who previously took sick leave to avoid working with the patients, now expressed a desire to work there. Dr. Hew Len continued his work at the hospital for almost four years, and eventually, only a few patients remained, and even they were cured. As a result, the Hawaii State Hospital was eventually shut down, as there were no more patients in need of treatment. **Sounds miraculous, right!**

Certainly, the Ho'oponopono prayer is often regarded as a miraculous practice. Now, let's dive deep into this remarkable prayer and explore how Dr. Hew Len was able to heal patients without even meeting them in person.

The term "Ho'oponopono" originates from "Ho'o" (meaning "to make") and "pono" (meaning "right"). The repetition of "pono" emphasizes the concept of being "doubly right" with oneself and others. Ho'oponopono is an ancient Hawaiian spiritual practice that encompasses the idea of accepting "Total Responsibility" for everything that exists in our surroundings. It involves acts of confession, repentance, and reconciliation as a means of learning to heal all aspects of life.

We all possess free will and are responsible for our choices and actions. It's essential to understand that I am not answerable for the choices made by others, except in situations where I have direct responsibility. Dr. Hew Len followed the key principle of taking total responsibility, which means that everything happening around us is a result of our own attraction. This includes the good, the bad, the worst, problems, sufferings, and all emotions that come our way. In the case of prisoners, he initially assumed responsibility for all of them, recognizing that if they are criminals and mentally ill today, it signifies that a part of himself is also responsible. This understanding arises from the fact that everything in the universe is composed of energy, and at the energy level, we are all interconnected as one.

When we understand the concept of being responsible for everything, we experience a sense of relief. This brings us to the four powerful sentences of Ho'oponopono, introduced by Dr. Hew Len:

1. "I am sorry."

2. "Please forgive me."

3. "Thank you."

4. "I love you."

As it is practically impossible to meet the prisoners in person, Dr. Hew Len took the register of patients and contemplated each and every name, taking 100% responsibility for their mental stress and the criminal acts that they had committed. This understanding delves into a profound healing process for our thoughts, feelings, and emotions at an atomic level. Let's consider an example: when we encounter someone who is injured or has been in an accident, what is our initial reaction as a typical person? Take a moment to think about it. Usually, we might feel a sense of pity or think, "Oh no! That poor person had to endure so much."

However, unknowingly, our thoughts contribute to the amplification of their pain, frustration, and hurt. By practicing the magical sentences, we address and cleanse these emotions that arise within us when witnessing others in such situations. It serves as a process of purification.

Positive energy flows in, and as we clear away negativity, things start to improve, leading to the occurrence of miracles. Many people have shared their stories of experiencing the transformative power of Ho'oponopono. That's why I refer to it as a "miraculous healing" process.

In the book *The Secret Prayer*, spiritual guru Joseph Vitale emphasizes the importance of forgiveness for both us and others. He explains that without forgiveness, we remain trapped in unconscious patterns and repetitive life experiences. Sometimes, knowingly or unknowingly, we may harm others or ourselves. Apologizing and seeking forgiveness become powerful tools for cleansing negative energy.

To put it simply, it's like wiping clean everything written on a slate and starting anew to create a beautiful life. How many of us have wished for a fresh start after making a mistake! Although we cannot change the past, uttering the sincere phrase "I am sorry" can work wonders in healing and transforming our lives.

1. This is an extension of the phrase "I am sorry." Asking for forgiveness reflects humility and shows that we are willing to take action to correct our mistakes. Before seeking forgiveness from others, it is essential to forgive ourselves. Often, when we say "yes" to others out of peer pressure or concern for their feelings, we unintentionally say "no" to ourselves.

2. Gratitude is of utmost importance. It involves being thankful to our inner self, expressing appreciation towards others, and acknowledging the greater creator for everything. It's essential to show gratitude not only for the good things but also for the challenges and difficult experiences we encounter. Every event in our lives has a purpose, even if we may not immediately comprehend it. Trusting in the perfect timing of the universe is crucial.

On a higher level, expressing gratitude to the universe or the almighty strengthens our faith. It shifts our subconscious mind from a state of complaint to a state of gratitude. The underlying principle is that what we focus on, we attract.

We all use the word "love" frequently in our daily lives, but have you ever pondered its deeper meaning? Just like anger, hate, happiness, sadness, sorrow, and excitement are emotions, love is also an emotion. However, many of us limit the concept of "love" to romantic partners, associating it solely with intimacy. But that's not the case. Love can be felt for anyone, regardless of our relationship with them. We can love our parents, siblings, friends, animals, and even non-living things. Love is a profoundly positive word that holds the power to resolve many complications simply by being spoken. Imagine the impact of expressing love wholeheartedly - it truly works like magic. (Further insights on love will be explored in the relationship chapter.)

Well, the beauty of the Ho'oponopono prayer is that we can use it anytime, anywhere, and for anything or anyone. You can say it to your relationships, boss, company, school, money, tensions, problems, or even objects like a pen, book, or laptop. The purpose is to clear negative frequencies. As we have learned earlier, when our frequency aligns with our goals, we attract positive things.

Exercise

Here is a simple Ho'oponopono prayer that you can recite daily or whenever you feel low and distressed. Our parents are the source of our very existence, providing us with love, compassion, patience, and everything we need. However, as we grow up, we may become disconnected from this source due to work, misunderstandings, or other reasons. Even if a person has wealth and social status, a strained relationship with their parents can create a lingering glitch. Now, let us work together to remove this blockage and bring healing.

Ho'oponopono to Parents:

I am sorry, Papa and Maa, for troubling you so much. I apologize for not giving you enough time and attention. I am very sorry, Papa, for not always obeying your words and for the times I have lied to you. I apologize, Maa, for not being able to talk to you as much as before, and for getting too busy with work. I am sorry, Maa, for taking you for granted. Papa, I apologize for being judgmental about your decisions. I regret bothering you to put me in a bigger college, and I am sorry, Papa, for getting angry with you. I apologize, Papa and Maa, for all the mistakes I have made from my early days until now.

(Note: Since I don't have access to personal information about you and your parents, I used generic terms "Papa" and "Maa" to replace actual names.)

Apologies and Forgiveness

Dear Papa and Maa, I humbly ask for your forgiveness for all my mistakes. Please forgive me for the times I have been rude to you, for lying, and for taking your love and care for granted. I deeply regret not always obeying your words. I am truly sorry for any pain or hurt I may have caused. Your understanding and forgiveness mean the world to me.

Thank you, Papa and Maa, for being there with me during my toughest times. Thank you so much for having faith in me when no one else believed. I am grateful for your anger towards me and the love you have showered upon me. Thank you, Papa and Maa, for shaping my life so beautifully. Even when I was a little boy/girl and no one understood my language, you were the ones who understood my unspoken words. Maa, thank you so much for cooking such delicious cuisine every time. And Papa, thank you so much for getting me everything even before I asked for it sometimes. There were times when you came back from the office, tired, but you always prioritized us kids and did so much for us.

I love you, Maa and Papa, for being with me all the time. You are my strength, and I am so grateful for the wonderful life you've given me. Thank you for always prioritizing me and making sacrifices to provide the best education. I simply love you, Maa and Papa, for everything - for being my parents, for loving me unconditionally, and for always adoring me. Your love means the world to me.

Activity:

(NOTE: Do not skip this activity, trust me, you are going to experience magical results if you religiously follow it)

After reading the story above, you might have questions about how to incorporate this prayer into our daily lives, especially if we are not facing mental illness or have a criminal background. You might be wondering who can chant this prayer and to whom should we say it. You might also be curious about how many times you should say it in a day, and so on. Let's explore these aspects further to understand how we can benefit from this powerful practice.

The answer to all these questions is simple. There's no need for a special day to feel gratitude; being alive itself is a special reason to be grateful to the creator. You can choose to pray 108 times, as explained in the previous chapter about the significance of 108. However, you can chant it as long as you feel the need to. Simply focus on the person, thing, place, or emotion you want to resolve conflicts with, or if you want to accomplish certain tasks, or if you want to strengthen a connection or bond. The power of this prayer lies in its flexibility and universality, making it accessible for anyone, anytime, and for any purpose.

Below, I am listing a few topics. Take the time to note down the Ho'oponopono prayer for each of them.

1. Parents (Our source) - "Dear Papa and Maa, please forgive me for any mistakes I've made and thank you for your unconditional love and support. I love you both so much."

2. Health (To God for keeping us healthy) - "Thank you, God, for blessing me with good health and well-being. I am grateful

for every breath I take and for the ability to enjoy life to the fullest."

3. Workplace (For providing sustenance) - "Thank you, Universe, for the opportunity to work and for providing sustenance for me and my family. I am sorry for any conflicts or negative energy I may have contributed, and I seek forgiveness."

4. Spouse (If married, or pray for the most compatible partner) - "Thank you, Universe, for bringing such a loving and supportive partner into my life. I am sorry for any misunderstandings or hurt I may have caused, and I am grateful for our beautiful connection."

5. This Book (For enriching us with knowledge) - "Thank you, author and the Universe, for this wonderful book that has enriched my knowledge and understanding. I am grateful for the insights it has provided me."

Chapter 5
Setting Up Goals:

Goals give life direction. They turn vague wishes into a route on a map, so your days add up to something that matters to you. When you define what you want – whether it's emotional security, creative fulfilment, steady income, or service to others – your choices become clearer and your energy gets channelled instead of scattered. Goals are the difference between moving and arriving.

What life looks like without goals

- **Days blur into routines.** Waking, working, scrolling, sleeping becomes the default loop and the feeling that time is "just passing" grows.
- **Small urgencies crowd out the important.** Reacting to emails and chores replaces building skills, relationships, or long-term projects.
- **Meaning drifts.** People can still be kind and productive, but without a guiding aim, achievements feel incidental rather than owned.

Example: A teacher who loves storytelling spends evenings bingeing shows instead of writing the children's book she's always imagined. Years pass, and the story never leaves her notebook.

How to set goals with clarity

1. **Identify your purpose**

- Notice what consistently energises you and what feels like obligation. Purpose lives at the intersection of passion, talent, and contribution.
- Quick check: when have you lost track of time because you were absorbed and happy? That points to purpose.

2. **Make a goal list from that purpose**
   - Write 3–7 goals that flow from your purpose. Include at least one short-term (3 months), one medium-term (1–2 years), and one long-term (5+ years).
   - For each goal, name **why** you want it and **what** you will actually do next. Keep actions concrete.

3. **Use the two W's for every goal**
   - **Why** – your deeper motivation, e.g., "I want financial stability to free my time for volunteering."
   - **What** – the specific steps: "Take a certification, save 20% monthly, apply for three jobs in the field."

Example: Purpose – "Help children learn to read." Goals – short: volunteer weekly at a library; medium: complete a child-education course; long: start a community reading centre.

Real motivations behind big numbers

Wanting to earn ₹1 crore per month means different things to different people. Translate big numbers into real needs:

- **Security** – cover essentials, protect family, never fear sudden crises.

- **Freedom** – buy time to travel, create, or leave a job you dislike.
- **Impact** – fund projects, hire people, or donate at scale.
- **Status and Validation** – feel recognised for capability and effort.

Example variants: One person aims for ₹1 crore to build a school; another wants that income to secure three generations; a third wants it as proof they overcame poverty. All are valid, and each needs different plans.

How the core human needs guide goal choices

Your five simplified priorities map naturally to why goals matter:

- **Love and Connection** – goals that protect relationships and create time for people you care about.
- **Contribution to Society** – goals aimed at service, charity, mentoring, or building community.
- **Personal Growth and Self-Development** – goals for learning, skill-building, and expanding capacity.
- **Sense of Importance and Self-Esteem** – goals that give you visible competence, recognition, and roles that matter.
- **Comfort and Security** – financial targets, health routines, and plans that reduce uncertainty.
- Design goals that balance these needs. A single-minded pursuit of money can neglect connection; a focus only on comfort can stall growth. The healthiest goal-sets include at least one objective from different needs.
- **Practical checklist to get started**

- Write a one-sentence purpose statement.
- List 3–7 goals linked to that purpose.
- For each goal, write the Why and the What (next 3 concrete actions).
- Assign a realistic timeframe and a simple metric of progress.
- Schedule one weekly check-in with yourself to adjust and celebrate small wins.
- Choose motion that feels meaningful, not just busy. Goals are not iron cages; they are maps you redraw as you learn, grow, and care for others.

Human needs can be categorized into two main types: basic or proximal needs, and distal needs related to personal development.

Proximal human needs are the fundamental necessities required for survival, such as food, water, and shelter. They also encompass elements like love from family and friends, peace to avoid violence or threats, and safety to prevent accidents.

On the other hand, distal human needs are essential for personal growth and self-development. These include learning and education, self-expression, recreation, personal growth (such as improving skills or personal appearance), and spiritual growth.

To achieve these needs effectively and easily, it's crucial to set clear goals and focus on them. Understanding the "what" and "why" behind our goals makes the process of "how" to achieve them more manageable.

When we have desires, they can merely be wishes if we don't take action. However, when we actively pursue and work towards our desires, they become real goals.

By choosing to read this book and seeking personal enrichment and learning, you already have a specific aim in mind. Don't let it stay as a mere wish; turn it into your goal and take concrete steps to achieve it.

SETTINGS GOALS IS THE FIRST STEP IN TURNING INVISIBLE INTO VISIBLE – Anthony Robbins

The key to setting and realizing our goals is simple: first, you must have a clear understanding of what you want to achieve in your life. Take the time to define your goals. Our priorities shape our identity and determine who we become. Each person's fundamental needs may differ. For some, money holds utmost importance, while for others, relationships take precedence, and so on. However, the truth is that we need a balance of everything. We require good health and financial stability to lead a luxurious life with our loved ones by our side. Who doesn't aspire to be respected, socially well-adjusted, and recognized?

Activity:

Identify

1. What ignites you?

2. What do you want from life?

Five years from now, how do you envision yourself? These questions will help you determine your goals and life's purpose. Take a moment to write down your goals in the three areas of your life: health, career, and relationships, which you aim to achieve within the next year.

Let's consider an example:

Health: To achieve fitness and overall well-being, maintaining a strong immune system and reaching my ideal body weight of ___ kg.

Career: To double my current earnings, reaching ___ per month, and securing a promotion that brings recognition, respect, and happiness with ease.

Relationships: To strengthen my bond with my parents and friends, creating deeper connections and nurturing meaningful relationships. If I am not married, to find an understanding and compatible life partner who shares my values and aspirations. If I am married, to foster a loving and caring relationship with my spouse, characterized by trust, communication, and deep intimacy. Moreover, to establish a strong and loving bond with my children, providing them with love, support, and guidance as they grow.

In the space below write down your goals:

So far, we have accomplished two crucial steps. By identifying and writing down our goals, we have strengthened our commitment to achieving them. Alongside, there are several powerful techniques like Nikola Tesla's 555 method, the magic of 1111, visualization, water bottle manifestation, and more. In this section, we will explore two techniques in-depth, which act as catalysts in manifesting our goals. These methods align us with the universe and train our subconscious mind. Now, let's move on to the third step: taking action towards our desired goals, engaging all our senses in the process.

We have five fundamental senses: smell, touch, taste, sight, and hearing. Additionally, our sixth sense, intuition, comes to life when we practice meditation and align with chakra healing.

Every person is unique, and we each have our preferred senses for connecting with the world. Some of us form strong associations through smell, which can evoke memories of beautiful moments. To determine if you are a visual person, try describing a party to a friend and see if you can recall even the tiniest details, such as what your friend was wearing, the colors of the table and curtains, or the brand name of a bag. If you can easily remember these details, then you are likely a visual person. The same principle applies to our other senses as well.

Visualization Technique

Visualization is a powerful technique that engages our sense of sight and can help us achieve our goals. To practice visualization, take a large cardboard and paste photos that represent your desired outcomes. For example, you can use images of yourself being fit and healthy, a smiling face, a joyful family holiday, bank account statements showing doubled increments in salary, and a picture of yourself in a state of happiness and peace. Attach affirmations to each photo, reinforcing the positive impact you want to create.

Consistently visualizing these images and affirmations helps train our subconscious mind, instilling belief in ourselves and the universe's support. With faith and belief, we become motivated to work diligently towards turning our visions into reality. Make it a daily practice to reinforce these positive images and affirmations, and you will see remarkable progress towards your goals.

THE JOY OF A FULLILLED LIFE
WORLD TOUR IN BUSINESS CLASS
EXCELLENCE AWARS
CAREER & RECOGNITION
EXCELLENCE AWARD
LOVING FAMILY
GOOD
FRIENDS
BEST-SELLER BOOK SIGNING
WEALTH ABUNDANCE
MULTIPLE BE INCOME
DREAM HOME
FINANCIALLY INDEPENDENT
I FEEL BEAUTIFUL & BLESSED

2. Water Bottle Technique:

Words hold incredible power as they vibrate with specific energy when spoken or written. We have witnessed the transformative effects of this power through ho'oponopono healing. The water bottle technique harnesses a similar concept, and there are two approaches to using it.

a) To observe quick results, focus on one small goal at a time. Take a glass of water and recite affirmations related to that specific area of your life. Each time you drink water during the day, direct your gaze towards the water, verbalize the affirmations, and genuinely feel and believe them. Embrace the conviction that as the water enters your body, you have already achieved your desired outcome. Experience the happiness and sense of accomplishment.

b) Another approach is to write down the affirmations and affix them to your water bottle. Leave the water bottle overnight, allowing it to become charged with the energy of the affirmations. The next morning, drink the water from the same bottle, absorbing the positive energy of the affirmations.

How does this technique work? You might be wondering why it is effective despite not physically mixing anything into the water. The answer lies in a simple and fundamental concept: we and the universe are not separate entities. Everything in the universe is composed of energy and vibrates at specific frequencies. When we grasp this understanding and communicate our affirmations to the water, we are essentially charging the water and aligning its vibration with the frequency of our desired outcome. As this charged water enters our body, filled with positive thoughts and affirmations, our subconscious mind is set in motion, working towards our goals, and the universe receives the message that the work has already been accomplished. In a way, it's like a signal sent to the universe, which responds by supporting us in manifesting our desires.

This concept is not a recent discovery; it has been known since the time of our ancestors. Perhaps you recall our grandparents advising us not to cry while eating. This was because unintentionally, we were negatively charging the food. Similarly, traditions across religions emphasize the importance of remembering and expressing gratitude to a higher power for providing us with sustenance, treating it as a sacred offering (prasadam). These ancient practices acknowledge the power of our thoughts and intentions, understanding that what we put out into the world comes back to us. By being mindful of our actions and infusing them with positive energy, we create a harmonious flow of abundance and blessings in our lives.

Activity:

In the space below, paste a photograph of your water bottle with affirmations pasted on it, or create your own vision board by cutting and pasting images that represent your desired outcomes. This will serve as a powerful reminder of your goals and intentions, reinforcing them in your subconscious mind and aligning your energy with the frequency of your aspirations. Keep this visual representation somewhere you can easily see it daily, allowing it to inspire and motivate you towards achieving your dreams.

Chapter 6
Affirmations

Affirmations are like powerful self-talks that have a direct impact on our subconscious mind, influencing our thoughts and actions in achieving success in different areas of life. It's crucial to be conscious of the content we feed into our subconscious.

Now, let's take a moment to ponder the following question: Imagine you have extraordinary superpowers that allow you to obtain anything you desire. What would be at the top of your list? Take some time to reflect and identify your deepest desires and aspirations. These will be the foundation of the affirmations you create to manifest your dreams into reality.

Now, did you envision pain, sorrow, irritation, hatred, or disrespectfulness when contemplating your desires? Most likely not. Just as we cannot wish such negativity upon others, it is inconceivable to desire it for ourselves. However, the harsh truth is that throughout the day, 24/7, we have a constant internal dialogue, like a repetitive recorder, that tends to focus on the negative aspects of things. We find ourselves saying things like, "Something bad shouldn't happen," "I shouldn't get stuck in traffic," or "I do not want to be late." These thoughts unintentionally send the wrong message to our subconscious mind.

Our mind does not comprehend words like "NO," "DO NOT," or "SHOULD NOT." So, every time we say, "I should not get late," our mind receives the message, "I should get late." If you observe closely, you will realize instances where you have said, "What I was scared of actually happened!" This is not a mere coincidence; it is you who manifested it. An example of such manifestation out of fear can be seen during the recent Covid-19 pandemic, where many people, in their fear of contracting the virus, actually succumbed to it. It highlights the significant role our thoughts and emotions play in shaping our reality. So, it becomes crucial to shift our focus from negative self-talk to positive affirmations and intentions, thus empowering ourselves to manifest the life we truly desire.

Our thoughts possess immense power. Even a person on their deathbed, given a prognosis of two days, can regain their health and live happily for many years. Conversely, a person who is not infected may lose their life due to their own internal tornado of negativity. It showcases the remarkable influence our thoughts and mindset have on our well-being and the course of our lives. It is a reminder that we must be mindful of our thoughts and choose positivity, as it can be a driving force in overcoming challenges and bringing about positive changes in our lives.

Things we should NEVER express to the universe:

1. Avoid making generic requests for an unspecified number of things. For example: "Some money," "many chocolates," "some good people in life," etc.
2. Refrain from complaining or lamenting about things. For example: "Why do I always have to suffer?" "I have so many problems." "I never look good at functions." "Why do I always face problems during my presentations?" "My company never gives me a raise," etc.

3. Never place blame on someone else for the situations or crises you are experiencing. For example: "It's because my mother-in-law shouted at me that my mood was spoiled the whole day." "My boss didn't appreciate me, so I didn't give the presentation the next time." "I am suffering because they didn't do their work properly," etc.

By avoiding these negative expressions, we can direct our energy towards positive and constructive thoughts, manifesting a more abundant and fulfilling life.

"Talk to yourself once in a day, otherwise, you may miss meeting an excellent person in this world."

1. Now that we understand what we should not express to the universe, let's simplify what we should tell ourselves or the universe:
    a) Focus only on what you want.
    b) Imagine that you already have it.
    c) Feel the experience of having it.
    d) Believe in its manifestation.
2. Refrain from expressing to the universe that you want something to happen. Instead, use positive affirmations to state that your desires have already been fulfilled. For example:
3. Be present in the joy and fully embrace the happiness of attaining what you desire. If you find it challenging to believe or perceive it as unrealistic, you can engage in activities like brisk walking, cardio exercises, or even dancing and jumping. These activities stimulate the release of happy hormones, and when combined with affirmations, they enhance the experience even further. If you still find yourself questioning, thinking, "How can I say I already have it when I actually want it?!" you must decide whether you want to rely solely on logic or if you're open to experiencing the magic of the universe! I am confident that we all desire magical and mystical experiences in our lives!
4. **Just "Feel it till you make it!"**

   And you'll be amazed by the results you achieve! By combining the three points mentioned above, we are now ready to create perfect affirmations.

   - Universe, thank you so much for granting me my ideal body weight of ___ kgs.

- Dear God, I am filled with joy and gratitude for my promotion as _____ in ____ company.
- Thank you, universe, for blessing me with a harmonious and fulfilling marriage to a partner who is physically fit, mentally strong, and financially stable, and who loves, understands, and cares for me deeply.

And so on... Once you grasp this technique, you can easily create affirmations for anything you desire. Embrace the power of these affirmations and experience the transformation they bring into your life!

Exercise: Using the examples provided above, write down five affirmations each for health, career, and relationship goals.

Chapter 7
FOCUS!! FOCUS!! FOCUS!!!!

The word "focus" has an interesting origin, stemming from the Latin word "focus," which originally meant a "fireplace" or "hearth" - the central area around a fireplace. When the word entered the English language around 1635-1645, it carried this primary connotation. However, over time, the use of the word evolved, and its original association with the fireplace gradually diminished.

Over time, the word "focus" continued to evolve and take on new meanings. During the 17th century, with the emergence of scientific literature written mainly in New Latin, "focus" gained further significance. The influential English philosopher and writer, Thomas Hobbes, used "focus" in the 1650s to describe a fixed point in geometry. Similarly, in the 1690s, the renowned scientist Isaac Newton also utilized the term in his work on gravity and optics.

During the late 1600s, "focus" found additional applications in the fields of medicine and physics. In physics, a focus refers to "a point where rays of light, heat, or other radiation converge after being refracted or reflected." It is easy to see how the concept of a fireplace or hearth, as a concentrated source of heat and light, became analogous to such a point in mathematical and scientific contexts. The word "focus" had now expanded its reach into various disciplines, symbolizing the central point of convergence or attention.

Dig deeper

The word "focus" acquired multiple meanings in the field of optics, particularly referring to "the point where rays converge or diverge on a lens." Another common sense of focus is "the state of a clear and sharply defined image, without blur." Optics has also introduced the expressions "in focus" and "out of focus," which can be used both literally and figuratively. In the literal sense, it relates to the clarity of an image formed by a lens, while in a figurative sense, it pertains to the level of attention and concentration given to a particular subject or task.

THE GREATEST SKILL ONE CAN DEVELOP IS DECREASING THE TIME BETWEEN IDEA AND EXECUTION.

The formula 2W+H+A=S stands for "What, Why, How, and Action leads to Success." It's a powerful tool to guide us in setting and achieving our goals. Define what you want, understand why you want it, plan how to achieve it, and take consistent action. This formula will lead you to success!

The formula for success, 2W+H+A=S, consists of the 2 "Ws" - What and Why, and the "H" - How. Understanding what we want to achieve and why we want to achieve it provides clarity and purpose, making it easier to plan how to execute our goals. However, having a clear plan is not enough on its own; taking action is crucial. By writing down our goals and plans, we maintain a clear flow of thoughts and increase our commitment to achieving them. Taking small steps towards our goals each day can lead to significant progress over time.

In our busy lives, we often follow a repetitive routine - waking up, having breakfast, going to work or school, and returning home to watch TV. It is essential to break out of this monotonous cycle and actively pursue our dreams and aspirations. By applying the 2W+H+A=S formula and taking consistent action, we can transform our lives and move closer to our desired outcomes.

Sometimes, we experience moments of relative stillness, yet we fail to utilize this time for self-reflection. These moments offer us an opportunity to contemplate our aspirations and the life we want to lead. What are our desires? Do we seek financial abundance or dream of exploring the world? These are some common examples of life goals.

Regarding human needs, it is essential to understand and categorize them into two types: basic needs and distal needs.

Basic human needs are fundamental for survival and well-being. They encompass necessities like food, water, and shelter, as well as emotional elements like love from family and friends, a sense of peace to avoid violence, and safety to prevent accidents.

In contrast, distal human needs are crucial for personal development and growth. They include pursuits such as learning and education, self-expression, engaging in recreational activities, self-improvement in various skills, enhancing personal appearance, and exploring spiritual growth.

Setting goals and maintaining focus are key factors in achieving our aspirations more effectively and effortlessly. Clarity on "What" we want to achieve and "Why" we desire it lays the foundation for determining "How" we will reach our goals.

Chapter 8
Self-Acceptance – Self Love

Before we dive into this intriguing topic, let's recognize a fundamental truth: each of us is born alone and will ultimately face death alone. Throughout this life's journey, the one constant companion is "Myself or I."

Every person on Earth possesses a unique identity. Even twins have distinct fingerprints, and no two individuals share the same DNA. Every being in this vast universe is intricately created by a divine force, with the essence of the Supreme Power residing within all of us. This concept holds true both scientifically and spiritually. Considering that we are handpicked and brought into existence by the ultimate creator, how can we harbor self-hatred? There should be no room for self-doubt.

Many times, we fall into the trap of self-hatred due to external factors like the non-acceptance or lack of validation of our thoughts and ideas by others. We may also experience guilt or regret for past actions. However, dwelling on these negative emotions only nurtures self-deprecation within us.

Why is it crucial to respect, love, and accept ourselves? This question carries immense significance as it enables us to value our existence fully, and in turn, has a positive impact on the people around us.

It is vital to prioritize self-nurturing with love, kindness, compassion, and self-esteem rather than seeking validation from others. Imagine yourself as a pot filled with water - only by filling yourself with positive emotions can you share them with others. Embracing self-love and acceptance will naturally attract positive energy from those around us.

The priority and importance we assign in life are determined by our desires and aspirations. When we hunger for success, our passion is directed towards our work. If we crave financial abundance, we focus on enhancing our skills to increase earnings. Similarly, if we long for popularity and fame, we seek to stand out and socialize. Now, here's an intriguing proposition: what if I told you that everything can be achieved by starting with loving yourself? Self-love acts as a catalyst, elevating our confidence to new heights and playing a crucial role in maintaining stability and promoting good mental health.

EVERYTHING
STARTS WITH YOU

How we treat others is a direct reflection of how we think about and treat ourselves. For example, if we constantly dislike someone for being angry, untidy, child-like, or lazy, it indicates that we harbor similar feelings towards those aspects within ourselves.

We cannot change others; if we seek to correct or improve something, we must initiate the change within ourselves. It's like trying to clean a dirty face by repeatedly wiping the mirror—it won't result in a clean face, will it? So, what is the ultimate solution? It's simple! Cleanse your face, and the reflection will automatically become clearer. In other words, by working on ourselves, we can influence positive change in our interactions with others.

Embracing self-acceptance is key. Accept yourself fully, including both your positive and negative attributes. Take 100% responsibility for all your actions. Be the kind of person you wish to attract. Embrace all aspects of yourself—whether it's being irresponsible, overweight, underweight, receiving low marks, obsessively clean, calculative, manipulative, or any other quality. Every trait has its value, and it's important to have them in the right proportion. Knowing when and how to utilize each quality is crucial.

Self-awareness is crucial in understanding our own traits and tendencies. By recognizing and accepting all aspects of ourselves, we can work towards balancing our qualities and utilizing them effectively in different situations. This self-acceptance and understanding pave the way for healthier relationships with others as well.

Affirmations on Self Love:

- I love and accept myself for who I am. I am a happy soul.
- I trust in my abilities and intuition.
- I embrace change and adapt easily to new situations.
- Challenges bring out the best in me, and I welcome them with open arms.

- I am fearless and view failure as a stepping stone to success.
- With each breath, I inhale confidence and exhale fear, insecurities, and self-doubt.
- I believe in my capabilities, and I can achieve anything I set my mind to.
- I live in the present moment and have complete confidence in my future.
- I attract positive circumstances and like-minded, supportive people into my life.
- I freely accept compliments from others and genuinely celebrate their successes as well, knowing that we are all connected at the energy level.
- I am a unique and special individual, deserving of respect from others.
- I am enough and worthy just as I am.
- I do not seek validation from anyone, as my self-worth comes from within.
- No one can trouble me without my consent; I am in control of my reactions and emotions.
- I confidently approach and connect with strangers, fostering new connections with enthusiasm.
- I dream big and possess the strength to turn my dreams into reality.
- I am loved and respected by others for the person I am.
- The Universe supports me at every step, and I am never alone in my journey.
- Every cell in my body expresses gratitude for the wonderful life I live.

Chapter 9
Relationships!

"Love alone can rekindle life."

Henri Frederic Amiel

What do we mean by "RELATIONSHIP"?

Now, let's explore one of my favorite and most cherished topics: relationships. Relationships always hold the top spot on my priority list. They encompass the bonds we share with others in society, including our parents, relatives, siblings, friends, romantic partners, office colleagues, and even our connection with ourselves and the divine. The glue that binds us together is LOVE. Without love, the world would be as vast and empty as the sand and sea.

Love is the essence that binds us together, creating profound connections with others in society. Our relationships encompass the bonds we share with parents, relatives, siblings, friends, romantic partners, colleagues, and even our connection with ourselves and the divine.

In the presence of a higher power, love takes on a deeper meaning. It involves surrendering and accepting ourselves, experiencing a sense of insignificance compared to the grandeur of the universe. This realization leads to enlightenment, transcending our entanglement with material comforts.

Sometimes, even after achieving everything, we may still feel restless, yearning for something greater. It is then that we understand the significance of aligning with the universe. True peace is found in this alignment, where prayers, mantras, and religious practices from various backgrounds teach us the fundamental truth of unity and harmony with the divine.

"Dear God you are hero I am zero

I Am your Child kindly guide, holding me

You are everything I am Nothing

I surrender myself to you"

Love between parents and children is a remarkable bond, fueled by the extraordinary power of a mother to bring new life into the world, second only to God Himself. In our lives, parents hold a position next to the divine, providing the foundational support upon which we build the rest of our journey. They act as our roots, establishing the base of our existence. Our first experiences in the nurturing environment of our home become the source of valuable teachings, shaping our moral compass.

As we grow, we are molded by our parents into the individuals we become in the future. Their love and guidance blend with respect, and the values they instill in us remain ingrained throughout our life's journey. The connection we share with our parents is enduring and profound, shaping our character and influencing the paths we choose to take.

Love between siblings and a friend is a unique and cherished bond for each individual. They stand by us through both joyous moments and challenging times. Despite occasional conflicts and feelings of love or jealousy, our connection with them deepens over the years, leading us to make sacrifices for their well-being.

Now, let's not underestimate the role of love and affection in the workplace! While we work for a salary and fulfill our job responsibilities, it doesn't mean there isn't room for genuine care and camaraderie among colleagues. Building positive relationships at work can enhance productivity and create a supportive, enjoyable work environment.

No, our workplace is not merely a location where we spend a significant portion of our lives; it is an opportunity to find fulfillment and passion. When you love what you do and aim to make a positive impact on society, work becomes more than a daily routine—it becomes a source of inspiration. Your passion will drive you, making each day a rewarding experience.

In an article by Devashish Chakravarty published in the *Economic Times* on Dec 10, 2018, it is explained that while you may not control every aspect of your work environment or the people around you, you can take actions to trigger the release of "happiness hormones" in your brain, such as dopamine, oxytocin, serotonin, and endorphin. These hormones play a vital role in enhancing your well-being and overall happiness.

"Success hormones." Let us realize that ***the privilege to work is a gift, the power to work is a blessing, and the love of work is success! - David O McKay***

Love between Couples / love in Marriage:

What does love in marriage mean to you? Don't underestimate the significance of this question! While many may assume they know the answer, love in marriage transcends the mere responsibilities of having children and taking care of them. It encompasses a profound connection where respect, understanding, intimacy, and mutual well-being are vital components, among other things. Love between couples is more than a mere ritual to follow; it is a lifelong bond that requires nurturing and dedication.

Each person's priorities and preferences differ, and it is not fair to label someone wrong for valuing money or foolish for prioritizing love and respect. It all comes down to our individual needs. However, we must possess certain essential life skills to understand and connect with society, thereby enhancing our emotional intelligence. Together, we will identify any flaws and explore how we can contribute our best to nurturing our relationships.

"LOVE is composed of a single soul inhabiting two bodies." - Aristotle

Now that we comprehend how dedication to work can lead to satisfaction and happiness, let's acknowledge the importance of bonding with parents, siblings, friends, and other members of society. These connections play a crucial role in our lives and contribute to our overall well-being in various ways.

However, have you ever received proper guidance on how to navigate relationships with parents, bosses, in-laws, and even your soulmate? Unfortunately, this crucial aspect is not typically taught in schools or universities. As a result, we witness numerous conflicts between countries, broken marriages due to misunderstandings, strained relationships with in-laws, children growing distant from their parents, children finding faults in their parents, ineffective communication between parents and children, dominating bosses, unsupportive colleagues, and even complaints towards God or the universe. It seems like everyone is quick to blame others for their problems, and this complaining mindset becomes endless. It's essential to recognize that relationships require not only knowledge but also practice and analysis as a skill.

What if I told you that I have a surefire formula to help you build strong relationships with everyone?

First, let's make an effort to understand the underlying causes of any issues so that we can address them with absolute clarity. It is common for many of us to prioritize relationships at the bottom of our list, mistakenly believing that career and money are the most important factors. While there may be some truth to this notion, deep down, we all know that money alone cannot bring true fulfillment. Just like a well-prepared dish requires a perfect balance of ingredients, our lives require a balance of various elements, including relationships.

Initially, we tend to have smooth relationships where we care for each other and bring out the best in ourselves. This phase is often referred to as the honeymoon period, whether it's the first year of marriage or the initial weeks at a new workplace. We experience joy and happiness during this time, as we all will be in a race to impress each other, even when we are not comfortable doing something, we tend to do it.

However, as we spend more time together, we start noticing certain flaws and begin to voice complaints. We find ourselves asking each other, "Why don't you understand?" or "It's my mistake for expecting something from you!" If this sounds familiar in your fights with your spouse, then congratulations! I'm about to share something mind-blowing with you that will shed light on why you fight in the first place.

Understanding the root cause of your conflicts and knowing how to address them will make problem-solving much smoother and easier.

The complexity of any relationship is shaped by our own unspoken rules. These rules could be anything, like expecting gifts as they were given during the initial days, or feeling upset when one partner doesn't participate in household chores. Sometimes, the issue is relying too much on each other and feeling dissatisfied when needs isn’t met.

But here's a surprising fact: even though both partners may know why they are upset, there is a 50% chance of avoiding fights escalating to adverse levels if they communicate openly. The problem arises when we "think" the other person should understand our unspoken demands and meet them according to our expectations. This thought can be the spoiler and the first red flag that couples need to recognize.

We are all different individuals, so how can one partner know that the other wants to go out for dinner and is tired of cooking at home? And how can the other partner know that their spouse is overwhelmed with work and needs some "me time" and space? Unless you are a mentalist like the famous influencer Miss Suhani Shah, mind reading is not possible! But there is definitely a way to know what your spouse wants and a way to address it, and it works wonders in strengthening your bond.

The solution is simple: "speak out" to each other and understand that we don't have superpowers to read minds. To build a strong relationship, we must make an effort to know each other well. It's essential to ask for or express our needs openly and honestly. Communication plays a vital role, and surprisingly, it's a skill that is not taught in school. Often, we see examples of poor communication in daily soap dramas, and while we laugh at their sarcastic exchanges, we realize that we do the same in real life most of the time.

For instance, imagine you're relaxing on the couch one Sunday evening, sharing details about a party you attended, while your partner appears busy playing a video game without reacting or showing much interest in your story. Your first thought might be, "He/she is never interested in my stories; you are ignoring me." In such a scenario, you might get upset and leave the place or change the topic randomly, both of which can spoil your day.

Instead, you can say something like, "Hey, I had a great time at the party, and I'd love to hear about your day too. Can we talk after you finish playing the game?" By expressing your feelings calmly and respectfully, you open up the possibility for a meaningful conversation and avoid unnecessary conflicts.

Hope now you got my point!

Do not expect your partner or anyone else to read between the lines or understand hidden meanings in your words. Practice direct communication: "SIDI BAAT NO BAKWAS" (which means convey your message directly). Now that we've learnt the importance of clear communication, let's also be sensible about what we expect from others, whether it's our spouse, parents, kids, siblings, boss, or colleagues.

Let me ask you a simple question! If you were a teacher and you wanted your students to pass an exam, would you set an easy paper or a difficult one? Naturally, you would set an easy paper! And even before you set the paper, you would make them aware of the syllabus. It's as simple as that! This principle applies to the people you love and want to be loved by in return.

In relationships, it's crucial to express our needs and expectations clearly, just like giving someone the syllabus before an exam. When both parties understand each other's expectations, it leads to a smoother and more fulfilling relationship. Avoiding assumptions and openly discussing your desires and boundaries is the key to building stronger and happier connections with your loved ones.

Set easy rules.

What we have learnt so far!

Points, to remember it:

1. IDENTIFY YOUR RULES (your love language)

2. DROP OLD DIFFICULT RULES

3. SET EASY RULES

How to set easy rules?

For example:

If your partner finds it difficult to go shopping with you once a week, let go of that rule and create a new one: "I am happy going out once a month." If you've been expecting your spouse to prepare a cup of coffee in bed, but they are unable to, request a cup of coffee by 9 a.m. Sometimes, you can even prepare it for them. At the same time, communicate what you would be comfortable with if they were to do it.

Love is not a one-time task; it's an ongoing process-a "LIFE SKILL" that requires continuous effort. Both partners can win in love, and it's essential to prioritize each other's feelings every day. As you improve your communication, understanding, and flexibility in relationships, you'll find it easier to connect with anyone and everyone.

Stronger relationships are like strong roots that provide a stable foundation for all other aspects of life to fall into place automatically. When you cultivate healthy and open connections with your loved ones, it positively impacts every area of your life.

If your partner leaves a wet towel on the bed and it upsets you, it could be because of an unspoken rule you have about keeping the house tidy. To make things easier, you can create a new rule and say, "It's okay, I understand that you might not be used to doing all these chores. Even if you do half of them at your own pace, I am happy." Don't forget to express gratitude as well. You can say, "Honey, thank you so much for helping me clear the mess." Remember, expressing gratitude is important in strengthening relationships.

Gradually, we will explore our beliefs and distinguish them from reality. We'll also learn how our generalizations influence our perceptions and how to change beliefs for our benefit.

Understanding how conflicts arise requires examining events in two parts: the action and the reaction. Our reaction involves ranking people and situations based on our own rules, creating a narrative that adds drama to the event. However, this narrative can be negative and distort the true nature of what happened.

Now that you comprehend how our minds can deceive us and attract negativity, it's essential to be mindful of these tendencies.

Event/Incident	What actually the incident mean	Our Perception	Story
Wife asks husband to accompany her for shopping and a day out, but the husband declines, saying, "No, I am a little occupied. Can we go next week?"	Husband said "No" for shopping. As he is pre scheduled.	The wife feels that her husband doesn't love her anymore. She believes that his priorities lie elsewhere and not with her. She thinks he has changed a lot and doesn't care for her because he said "no" to going shopping..	Doesn't love me never cares for me; I am not his priority, changed a lot.

To understand what unwritten rules are, let me share some examples of so-called universally accepted rules we have created.

Please fill in the blanks below with two unwritten rules that others may have about you, and then write what you truly are or what you aim to be in the belief change box.

Universally accepted unwritten rules	Belief Change
Women take care of house, man is breadwinner and goes out to work.	Now it's the era of women, she is respected and given equal rights, remember the movie Ki and Ka! There are many such couples in real life too!
Sun rises in the east and sets in the west!	No, it's universally accepted where as we all know technically it's not the sun which moves. It's the earth which revolves around the sun!
Famous Hindi dialogue " Mard ko dard nahi hota," which means man is never hurt. Qualities of man are strength, power, toughness - come what may!	Truth is, "Mard ko bhi dard hota hai" - even a man feels sad, hurt, weak, low. It's absolutely normal to feel so.
Women are physically weak.	Not really. Women have joined the army, research centers, and do all challenging jobs with the same zeal and energy as men do.

These unwritten rules are also called generalization in the NLP technique.(Neuro-Linguistic Programming of our brain).

I have listed some universally accepted rules, and in addition to those, each one of us has our own set of personal rules for everything and everyone we encounter. These personal rules become the criteria by which we judge and evaluate our interactions and relationships. When these rules are not met or conflicts arise, our relationships can begin to strain. Let's delve deeper into this concept to understand its impact on our lives.

LOVE is a VERB: "Honey! I love you... and I mean it!" said a busy businessman, quickly returning to his laptop for more meetings and discussions. His lady was left wondering, was that even love? How did he mean it? He didn't do anything to make me feel loved! After contemplating for a while, she approached him and asked if they could talk or play carrom together, or even water the plants. However, all she heard in response was, "I'm busy right now, can we do it later?"

In this scenario, the businessman expressed love verbally, but his actions didn't align with his words. Love is not just a feeling or something we say; it is a verb, an action that we demonstrate through our deeds and behavior. It's about making time for each other, being attentive, and engaging in activities that nurture the bond. Love is both spoken and shown, and when it becomes a verb, it fosters a deeper and more meaningful connection.

Today, this is a common story for almost every second person. In primary school, we learnt about nouns, pronouns, verbs, adverbs, adjectives, and more. These are known as parts of speech. Without delving into too much detail, let's get straight to the point: what is a verb? It is a word that expresses action, such as breathing, running, dancing, and walking. "Love" is also an action. So, if you keep saying "I love you" to someone but ignore their calls, disregard their thoughts, rarely spend time with them, or fail to share your feelings, can the other person truly feel it? ABSOLUTELY NOT.

Love, as a verb, requires concrete actions and efforts to make someone feel cared for and cherished. Mere words without matching actions become meaningless. To truly express love, we must engage in acts of kindness, show appreciation, listen attentively, and be emotionally available. Love is an ongoing process of showing, demonstrating, and reciprocating affection, which strengthens the bond between two people. So, let's not just say "I love you" but also show it through our deeds and behavior.

Affirmation coupled with relevant actions towards our goals is what leads us to success. Similarly, simply saying "I love you" without any corresponding actions will have zero impact on your partner.

Love is not just a static declaration; it requires dynamic expressions through thoughtful gestures, genuine care, and active involvement in each other's lives. Instead of assuming that our feelings are understood, let's communicate openly and fulfill each other's emotional needs. Through meaningful actions, we can solidify the bond of love and build a relationship that thrives on mutual affection and support.

Words possess power, but their effectiveness amplifies when accompanied by action. Spending quality time together and engaging in meaningful conversations may not directly bring financial gains, but it nourishes our mental well-being and provides satisfaction by fostering connections with our loved ones. It's easy to overlook that love needs to be nurtured and recharged daily, much like charging a phone to keep it functioning.

Love is best expressed spontaneously, and the ways in which we express love vary for each individual. Remember how we used to memorize maths formulas, numerical tables, and chemistry equations without fully understanding their meanings? Similarly, I'll provide you with a list of ways to express love. It's

crucial to practice them consistently, regardless of whether they make sense to you or not, and even if you don't fully comprehend them. Embrace the mindset of "fake it till you make it," and trust me, you'll witness the desired results with certainty.

*Practice patient listening: By attentively listening to your spouse without immediately offering suggestions or guidance, you will experience transformative results in your relationships. The bond between you will strengthen, and your spouse will feel respected and valued.

1. Avoid arguments: Arguments can be detrimental to relationships. Instead, strive for healthy discussions where you can express your thoughts and opinions in a constructive manner.

2. Embrace the power of a warm hug: Just like the famous saying "An apple a day keeps the doctor away," a warm hug possesses remarkable healing power. Make it a daily habit to share a warm and comforting embrace with your loved ones. It has the ability to dispel misunderstandings and conflicts, fostering harmony and understanding.

Now; create any two expression of love for your beloved ones write down in the space below and practice it:

____

____

____

____

____

Love is a Feeling: Strengthen It Love is an emotion, a profound feeling that transcends words. To grasp its essence, observe the interaction between a newborn baby and their mother. Despite their inability to understand each other's language, their presence together evokes happiness and love. The baby expresses its affection through smiles, while the mother is overwhelmed with joy at the sight of her child. There is no need for any specific action; even the mere thought or presence of the baby is enough to evoke these emotions.

Similarly, in our relationships, we must nurture and strengthen the feeling of love. It's not just about saying "I love you" but also about showing it through our actions, empathy, and understanding. Like a delicate flower, love needs care, attention, and affection to bloom and thrive. So, let's water the roots of our relationships with love and watch them flourish with boundless happiness and fulfillment.

Think about the images of your loved ones that spontaneously came to mind as you read the previous paragraph. Reflect on the number of people who effortlessly entered your thoughts. Just the mere thought of them brings a smile to your face and triggers the release of oxytocin, the "love hormone."

These moments of connection and joy remind us of the deep emotional bonds we share with those we love. It's a beautiful reminder that love is not just a concept or a word; it's a powerful force that affects us at a physiological level. The simple thought of our loved ones can ignite a cascade of positive emotions within us.

Let's cherish these moments of love and appreciation, and let them motivate us to express our love and gratitude more often.

Whether through a heartfelt gesture, a warm hug, or a simple "thank you," let's strengthen the bonds with our loved ones and create a ripple effect of love and happiness in our lives.

Identify the love languages of five loved ones (acts of service, quality time, words of affirmation, physical touch, or receiving gifts) and note how often you fulfill them. Strengthen relationships by understanding and meeting their unique love languages. Show your love in ways that resonate with them.

Chapter 10
Relationships Banking Management (RBM)

Let's explore why and how relationships can be likened to banking. To understand this concept better, let's break it down in simpler terms.

Sure, let's begin by defining what a "bank" is. In simple terms, a bank is an institution that takes money deposits from the public and utilizes them to provide loans or make investments. These deposits are typically available for withdrawal whenever the depositors wish.

In essence, this concept revolves around the idea of debit and credit, similar to withdrawals and deposits. To conduct financial transactions with a bank, a person must open an account, which marks the initial stage of the banker-customer relationship.

Similarly, throughout our lives, we unknowingly establish an account with others, which can be referred to as our karmic account. From the moment we wake up in the morning to the time we go to sleep, we encounter numerous people, experiencing emotions such as sadness, anger, or blessings. Through these interactions, we either make debits or credits in our relationship with the people around us.

Let's understand this with an example: On a Monday morning, you arrive at your office and greet your boss with a cheerful "Good morning!" However, you notice that your boss does not respond with the same enthusiasm. Instead, they simply say "ok" and hand you a bunch of office files, instructing you to submit them within an hour. You start wondering what went wrong, as it's just the beginning of the day. You come to a random conclusion that your boss is never in a good mood or that your boss dislikes you, and so on.

However, the reality might be different. Maybe your boss is facing a personal issue or has a lot on their plate that day. Instead of jumping to conclusions and making negative assumptions, it's essential to communicate and clarify the situation. By doing so, you avoid unnecessary debits in your relationship with your boss and foster a healthier work environment.

An interesting fact to notice here is that the day you met your boss, your karmic account or relationship account was also opened! From that day onwards, every action and interaction you had with your boss counted. For instance, if you came up with a brilliant idea for a project and impressed your boss, it added to the credit in your account. Similarly, if you impressed clients with your presentation and gained recognition for your company, your boss felt even more positive about you, resulting in a larger credit (deposit).

However, there are also instances that can lead to debits (withdrawals) from your relationship account, such as coming late to the office without informing or ignoring a call from your boss. If there are more withdrawals than deposits in the account, it ends up with a negative balance. If the account is not nurtured, it can eventually become a Non-Performing Asset (NPA). In such a case, you will gradually notice a decline in your relationship, with a lack of interest in spending time together or sharing thoughts openly. It's crucial to be mindful of these interactions and strive to maintain a positive balance in your relationship account by nurturing it with care and understanding.

Indeed, it's not a sudden change in the other person's behavior. Instead, it's the cumulative effect of numerous withdrawals from the relationship account that eventually leads to such negativity. Small actions or lack of consideration over time can erode the trust and positivity in any relationship. Building strong relationships requires consistent efforts in making deposits of love, understanding, and care to ensure a healthy and thriving connection with others.

In our lives, we encounter situations where we feel a negative vibe when meeting someone for the first time. This feeling might stem from our karmic account with that person from a previous life. Similar to how you cannot close a bank account with a negative balance, in the realm of karma, you need to bring the account to zero by depositing positive actions and intentions. If you held grudges or negative feelings towards a soul in a previous life, that karmic account carries over to the next life. Our interconnectedness at the energy level allows us to sense these vibes and emotions.

Now, apply the RBM theory to all the people in your life - parents, siblings, spouse, friends, relatives, and observe where the accounting is turning negative. Assess if there are any slippages or non-performing accounts, or if there are healthy deposits of positive interactions. You might be surprised by the insights you gain through this exercise.

By honestly evaluating your relationships, you can accurately assess whether your marriage is facing challenges due to numerous withdrawals from the relationship. Similarly, you may realize that you've withdrawn more from your relationship with your parents, leading to a blockage in the connection.

Once you recognize these patterns, the next step is to take conscious actions to rectify the situation. Start depositing positive actions and intentions into your relationships. Communicate openly, express gratitude, and make efforts to improve your interactions with your loved ones. Just like in banking, with consistent nurturing, your relationship accounts will flourish, and you'll experience more positive and fulfilling connections with the people in your life.

It's very simple: now that you recognize the withdrawals you've made, it's time to start making deposits in your relationship accounts. You can begin by spending more quality time with your parents, actively listening to them, and understanding their love language to make them feel appreciated and loved. However, it's crucial to remember that while trying to improve relationships, you should never compromise your self-respect or authenticity.

Let's address a few common withdrawals that we often unknowingly make, underestimating their impact:

A) Ignoring: Not expressing yourself when it's expected can be a significant withdrawal. It shows that you are disregarding the other person's feelings, even if the matter may seem insignificant to you.

"Keeping calm and silent is good but when you are meant to open up and you are quiet, this will turn the table upside-down – It's a big NO NO"

B) Not listening: People, especially women, appreciate the opportunity to express themselves and share their problems. If your girlfriend or wife comes to you to talk about her issues, and you don't fully listen, but instead jump in with quick solutions, it's another withdrawal from the relationship account. It's essential to lend a supportive ear and show genuine interest in understanding her feelings and concerns.

You might think you're being helpful by providing solutions, as people, in general, tend to be practical problem-solvers. However, it's important to remember that each individual may need a different response. Your male best friend might require a different approach compared to your female best friend. For instance, women often know the solutions to their problems; they simply want to be heard, supported, and valued. Giving them your time and attention is what matters most to them, rather than immediately jumping in with solutions. Being an attentive and empathetic listener can make a significant positive impact on your relationships.

More such traits are elaborated upon by **John Gray** in his book –

"Men Are from Mars, Women Are from Venus."

In the space below list the **deposits** you can make with -

Hint: Gifting a small chocolate, Listening, respecting their viewpoint, making a cup of coffee, gifting someone our time by taking a day off etc.

Parents:

In-Laws:

Friend:

Spouse:

Relatives:

Boss:

Siblings:

Isn't it great to finally have this newfound understanding of our relationship dynamics? Now, we can accurately assess the areas where we may have made withdrawals and identify that we need to make 10 deposits to restore balance. By making even more deposits, we can not only bring the relationship back to normal but also cultivate a healthier and more fulfilling connection with our loved ones.

However, it's crucial to be mindful that making excessive deposits can lead the other person to take us for granted. Just like in banking terms, if an account is only credited without any debits, it is considered a partially frozen account. Therefore, maintaining a proper balance is essential. While we make deposits to nurture the relationship, it's also important to assert ourselves and be willing to withdraw when necessary. Setting healthy boundaries allows for a balanced and respectful connection with our loved ones.

"Relationship Banking Management runs

just as you run your savings bank account or current account

the more the deposits, more interest you acquire,

just as more you invest into your relationship the interest you acquire is priceless."

Chapter 11
Career and Wealth

Career And Wealth:

Wealth is Power.

Wealth is Respect.

Wealth is Luxury.

Wealth is Love.

What is your definition of Wealth??? What do you understand by being Rich? What is Money?

Let's start by understanding the meanings of these terms. Money serves as a medium for exchanging energy and acquiring goods and services. It represents our earnings received on a monthly basis. However, if one spends their entire salary of 1 lakh on a luxurious lifestyle, they may be considered rich but not truly wealthy. Wealth extends beyond one's salary and encompasses the assets accumulated through passive income. It involves owning assets that appreciate over time without requiring continuous personal effort. Therefore, instead of solely desiring riches, the goal should be to achieve wealth and financial freedom.

Can we really grow money?

Yes, it is true that we can make our money grow! However, the idea of money multiplying magically, like my grandmother's trunk, is just a fantasy. In reality, money grows through investment, not by simply saving or stashing it away. While it is essential to save money from our salary for emergencies, there are various options offered by banks such as recurring deposits and fixed deposits. For more detailed information on where to invest and how to save money, I recommend reading the book "Rich Dad Poor Dad" by Robert Kiyosaki and Sharon Lechter.

In this chapter, you will learn about effective money management and aligning your money frequency. It will help you understand why some people earn money easily while struggling with expenses.

Contrary to the belief that obtaining a university degree guarantees financial independence, we now see children earning money through diverse means such as the stock market, digital marketing, acting in movies, music, and more. It's evident that the earning potential is not solely determined by a degree but rather by the skill set one possesses.

Now, the crucial question arises: Is having a skill set the sole requirement to become wealthy? The answer is NO. While our skill set enables us to earn, achieving wealth and financial freedom requires something more: financial literacy.

Financial literacy entails understanding what is best for you and managing the money you earn in a way that allows your money to work for you and generate more wealth. It's about making informed decisions and leveraging your resources to secure a prosperous future.

1st level	Time for Money	All Employees, Source of income only 1-2. Income is defined. We work for Money
2nd Level	Money for Money	The savings done by Employees, from the salary, (earning interest from RD/FD/Gold bonds/Insurance, etc), Which is regarded as safe, and has less growth. We spend less to save the money.
3rd level	Money for Time	Employer, they bid money for time. Businessmen, Cricketers, Celebrities etc. Money works for us.

Take a moment to analyze which financial block you belong to. Many people find comfort in the first and second levels. The second level, in particular, is perceived as safer, as it minimizes potential losses. In numerous middle-class households, the common practice is to pursue education, earn a stable income, save for the future, and adopt a mindset that associates having too much money with risks. There is a prevailing belief that significant earnings must involve illegal activities or that making money is inherently difficult. These limiting beliefs create money blockages, acting as barriers that hinder our ability to earn more and achieve wealth. Consequently, many individuals spend their entire lives working for others, believing they are playing it safe, while their financial growth remains stagnant.

Let's analyze the two levels of our money mindset. In the first level, we often work for a company or institution, investing 8 to 9 hours of our day, and receive a fixed salary in return. This setup means we are essentially trading our time for money.

In the second level, we may not experience significant financial growth, but there is also a lack of sharp decline. Here, the focus is on saving earnings and minimizing unnecessary expenses. Sometimes, we might sacrifice our immediate desires to prioritize future security and manage to accumulate savings. This approach is commonly known as the "money for money" block.

The third block is known as the millionaire block! This category includes entrepreneurs, celebrities, and all the millionaires in the world. They prioritize time over money, recognizing the significance of time in their lives.

Now, let's turn our attention to dispelling limiting beliefs and inviting abundance into our lives. Our thoughts have the power to shape our destiny. Every significant event, invention, or accomplishment starts as a mere thought in someone's mind before it materializes into reality. The outcome hinges on the purity and positivity of our thoughts, propelling us towards achieving good, better, or even the best results.

Here are some essential steps to follow:

1. Identify your strengths and invest time in further developing them.
2. Don't wait for opportunities to come knocking at your door. Step out of your comfort zone and explore new avenues. When faced with obstacles, take a moment to reassess and then continue with even greater determination.
3. Instead of solely focusing on monetary gains, work selflessly to elevate global standards. By doing so, you will attract wealth, blessings, and the power to effortlessly draw love and fame. Comfort and abundance will naturally follow.
4. Remember, the power of your thoughts and actions can lead you to a successful and fulfilling life.

Chapter 12
Turning Pebbles to Pearls

In life, we often encounter situations where our efforts seem insufficient, and obstacles keep appearing, causing our trust to waver. We may wonder why our hard work doesn't yield the desired outcomes. If you find yourself in such a situation, there are usually two possibilities:

a) You may not be analyzing the situation objectively, leading you to only see the hurdles.

b) You may be limiting yourself to one narrow solution, which can create a blockage in your thinking.

Let's discover simple yet effective methods to smoothly overcome these situations, ensuring that the next time you face obstacles, you'll greet them with a sense of celebration! Yes, you read that correctly. This offers us the ideal remedy for the everyday tensions we encounter. The initial step involves staying calm and relaxed, reassuring yourself that problems only become influential when you pay them excessive attention.

- Now, you might be wondering how to accomplish that. It's achieved by deliberately redirecting your focus away from your problems. Instead of incessantly dwelling on them, we inadvertently continue to manifest and attract more problems into our lives. Even when everything else is perfect, our fearful thoughts behave like a boomerang – they keep returning to us.
- Our thoughts in distress–

- What if my manager rejects my project?
- What if I fail in my exam?
- What if I won't be able to pay my credit card bills?
- Will I be able to get my visa extension?
- My daughter scored fewer marks, just like last year.
- Why am I not finding the perfect match?
- I failed in this interview! I might not get any other good offers again. This was the only one, and I lost it.
- Why does he/she not love me the way I love them? Why am I being ignored by everyone?
- My parents never understand me.
- Why is it always me, God? Why do you ALWAYS put me into problems?

This is what is referred to as negative manifestation.

Why do we encounter such thoughts? It's normal to have negative thoughts, but fixating on them is not beneficial. Just as we address cough, cold, fever, and other illnesses, we should treat negative thoughts as if they were ailments. Just as we take medicine promptly when we have a high temperature or a cold, our negative thoughts also demand some form of remedy. We may not be able to entirely eradicate them, but we can overcome them.

Our new approach to handling distressing thoughts should be a remedy for our minds. Here are some affirmations for events that are yet to unfold:

- I have given my best effort to the project, and it is receiving appreciation. Thank you, universe.
- Thank you, universe, for guiding me to excel in my exam with outstanding marks.

- I am grateful for the miraculous ways in which I am earning from various sources of income, enabling me to pay my bills joyfully, just as I have done in the past.

And for events that have already occurred, we can use the following affirmations:

I love and accept myself just the way I am. Even though I didn't clear the exam, I still love myself and take responsibility for it. I am focused on improving and attracting abundance and peace in my work, relationships, and career.

Thank you, universe, for always being there to support me and for the challenges that have made me stronger. I am grateful for being chosen to overcome them.

Even the most expensive phone eventually runs out of power and becomes inactive. To keep it going, we charge it every day. Similarly, even the most challenging situations in our lives have an end. They become inactive after some time. It is we who continue giving them importance and keep them charged. So, what can we do instead?

3 things you can do:

I-A-S

Identify - Act – Surrender

The best approach is to write down the problem exactly as it is, which already solves 50% of the issue. Then, explore the possibilities and potential actions you can take. If there is something you can do about it, take action. For matters like exams, illness, marriage, salary hike, and others, sitting and lamenting won't bring any solutions. Instead, make affirmations and take steps towards your goals, moving closer each day.

The final step is surrendering. Even if you excel in everything, believing that it's solely your efforts carries a hint of ego. Acknowledge that the supreme power within you is constantly supporting you. Surrender to that power, and it will guide you on the right path. Surrendering has been my personal experience as the easiest and most powerful way to overcome any challenges. When you affirm something with the right intention, work towards it, and release doubts, fears, and anxieties, the universe works its magic. So, when you feel confused and uncertain, remember to I-A-S: Identify, Act, and Surrender.

b) The second approach to finding a solution to any problem is by altering your approach to the challenge. It may sound complicated, but it's actually quite simple. Just like every lock has a key, there is no problem in this world without a solution. Sometimes, when we focus on our goals, we create a blueprint in our minds on how to achieve them. However, when that plan doesn't work, we tend to give up. Instead, by changing our approach to life's challenges, we can attain ultimate supremacy. If Plan A is not working, remember that there are infinite other ways to accomplish your goals. As long as we don't give up, we are not considered losers.

Chapter 13
Overcoming the Fear of Death:

Experiencing a profound sense of numbness, as if the entire world has ceased to rotate, day and night appearing as a strange phenomenon, with no desire to eat, drink, or engage in any activity. Even breathing feels uncertain, and thoughts wonder why it had to be me. In such moments, the most common question anyone asks is, "Why did you take them away from me? It wasn't the right time; they were so young." And if the departed individual was older, we say we could have done everything possible to keep them alive. All of these emotions boil down to one thing: the fear of losing our loved ones.

Have you ever encountered such a situation before? What a seemingly obvious question to ask, isn't it? Because we all know it's an undeniable truth - every person who is born is bound to face death one day. The moment someone is born, the time, day, and date of their death are already predetermined. I'm not the one saying this! It's an unspoken rule of nature. The universe always maintains a balance between good and bad, yin and yang, happiness and sorrow, birth and death, and so on.

Losing a loved one is undoubtedly one of the most challenging experiences we have to face in life. Whether it's the loss of a parent, sibling, friend, or even a beloved pet, the emotional pain and grief can be all-consuming, and the healing process can be lengthy. In this article, we will explore the various stages of grief, offer strategies for coping with loss, and provide guidance on supporting someone who is grieving. Whether you are personally going through this ordeal or seeking ways to assist someone in their grief journey, this article will offer valuable insights and practical tips to navigate through this challenging period.

Section 1: The universal balance of good and bad

Section 2: The different stages of grief

Section 3: Coping mechanisms for dealing with grief

Section 4: Supporting someone who is grieving.

1. The Balance of Good and Bad in the Universe:

What does this concept of balance entail, and why is it crucial to grasp its significance? Without delving into complex scientific explanations, in simpler terms, it can be understood as follows: Just as we cherish a beautiful, sunlit day, we must also endure the darkness of night. If benevolent individuals come into our lives to aid and support us during our most trying moments, we can also expect to encounter a few negative and troublesome individuals along our journey. When we find ourselves in a state of suffering, we can anticipate being bestowed with gifts and moments of serenity. Similarly, when we joyfully embrace the arrival of a newborn into our lives, we must also prepare for the inevitability of death. This is how the universe maintains equilibrium and ensures balance in all aspects of existence.

But does that imply that the sun is good and the moon is bad? Is birth good and death bad? Not at all. It is crucial to grasp that nothing in the universe is inherently good or bad. The night possesses its unique qualities–it is a time for calmness and rejuvenation. Just as a restful night's sleep renews our body cells and prepares us for the next day, we can view it as a necessary process. Night is not permanent, and we can be certain that after a while, we will witness the return of sunshine.

Imagine if there were only the sun—could we work tirelessly without rest? It would be impossible. So what about the death of a person then? You might be wondering how death is inevitable and how it can be likened to the simple concept of day and night. I have a compelling reason, and it is a fact.

Consider water: when you freeze it, it transforms into ice, and if you boil that same ice, it evaporates and becomes a gas. Now, can you claim that water ceases to exist altogether? Of course not. Although it may not be present in its liquid state, it exists in the form of gas, and it can return to its liquid state again when it condenses into rain. Now you can relate our "SOUL" to water. Just as water transforms, our soul is born into and leaves one body, only to take up birth in new bodies subsequently. We all learned this basic concept in our early years of education. The fundamental idea is as straightforward as this: our universe itself is a vast university of life. "Sit with yourself, and you will discover the universe; explore the universe, and you will discover yourself." Life has no endpoint, which is why we refer to it as a life cycle.

When we experience grief, pain, and a sense of loss, we often feel as though a part of ourselves has died, as our loved ones are no longer physically present. However, you know what? It is merely the state of matter of our loved ones that has changed from a physical body to spirit. When you truly grasp this fundamental concept, you will feel a sense of joy, for your loved one has completed one life cycle and has transitioned into the spiritual realm. They are not confined to that spiritual state forever; they will be reborn, perhaps into a different family, just as water evaporates and returns in the form of rain.

The Different Stages of Grief – A Journey We All Walk

When we lose someone we love, the world doesn't just change outside us – it shifts inside us too. Psychologists like Elisabeth Kübler-Ross have described grief as unfolding in stages, but if you look closely, our own saints and epics have been whispering the same wisdom for centuries. Think of it less as a rigid sequence and more as waves that rise and fall, carrying us slowly toward healing.

1. Denial – *"This cannot be true."*

In the first days, the mind simply refuses to believe. You may wake up expecting to hear their voice, or glance at the door thinking they'll walk in. This is not foolishness – it is love clinging to form.

Remember Yudhishthira in the *Mahabharata*, stunned into silence when Abhimanyu fell. His heart could not accept that the radiant boy who entered the Chakravyuha would not return. Denial is that pause – the soul's way of cushioning itself before it can bear the full truth.

2. Anger – *"Why did this happen?"*

When the numbness fades, anger often takes its place. You may find yourself questioning God, blaming fate, or even feeling upset with the one who left. "Why did you go? Why me?" These questions are natural.

Even Arjuna, the great warrior, raged against destiny when his son was taken. Anger is not cruelty – it is love in its rawest form, demanding answers from a universe that feels unjust.

3. Bargaining – *"If only..."*

Soon, the heart begins to plead. "If only I had been there... If only I had prayed harder... If only God would take me instead." Bargaining is the mind's attempt to rewrite destiny, to strike a deal with the divine.

Think of King Dasharatha, who wished he could bear Rama's exile himself. Bargaining is that desperate wish to exchange places, to undo what has already been written.

4. Depression – *"I cannot go on."*

When bargaining fails, silence descends. The world feels colorless, and even the smallest tasks seem heavy. This is not weakness – it is the soul mourning deeply.

Kunti, after Karna's death, carried a sorrow that words could not capture. Her grief was not loud, but it was profound. Depression is that quiet valley where the heart learns the depth of its loss.

5. Acceptance – *"Life will never be the same, but I will carry on."*

Acceptance does not mean forgetting, nor does it mean the pain vanishes. It means learning to live with the absence, to carry the memory as part of your being.

As Krishna tells Arjuna in the *Bhagavad Gita*: *"For the soul there is neither birth nor death at any time... The soul is eternal."* Acceptance is this wisdom dawning within us – that while the body departs, love and spirit remain.

Think of grief as a river: at first, its current is wild and overwhelming. But as time passes, it begins to flow more gently, carrying with it both your tears and your love. You don't stop missing the one you lost — you simply learn to walk beside the river, instead of being swept away by it.

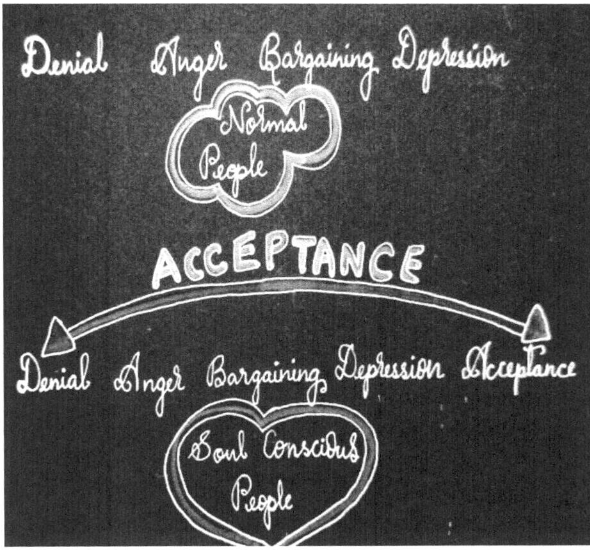

Now that we are aware that the pain we experience has four stages and gradually becomes lighter as we reach the fourth stage, it is important to comprehend how to cope with this phase of our lives and restore our energy and happiness.

Before we delve into finding solutions, it is crucial to recognize that it is foolish to believe that we cannot be happy in the future, and we should not feel guilty about choosing to smile and be happy.

The first crucial step is to handle anger and frustration in the right way. But what is the right way to manage anger? Anger is simply a surge of energy that can transform into tears when we feel helpless. To redirect this energy, we can engage in activities such as taking a walk, punching a bag, or expressing ourselves through singing or dancing. By doing so, we allow the energy to flow through our bodies, preventing it from converting into tears and emotional pain. Instead, physical activity releases hormones and boosts the production of feel-good neurotransmitters in the brain, such as endorphins. It is difficult to feel sad and depressed while engaging in activities like jumping or running because these actions require us to be in a different physical state.

For instance, when we slump our heads down, hold our foreheads, refrain from smiling, and remain seated in one place for extended periods, we send signals to our brains that can lead to a sense of paralysis and negative emotions.

Now that we are aware of these body language cues, we can take steps to improve our well-being by doing the opposite:

a) Change your body language: Lift your face and sit up straight, adopting a more positive and confident posture.

b) Engage in physical activities: Participate in activities that involve movement and exercise, as they can help uplift your mood and release endorphins.

c) Thirdly, and most importantly, avoid escaping from the memories of your loved one. Instead of forcing yourself to forget the pain and distracting yourself with other activities, embrace their memories and celebrate their deeds. Cherish the happy moments spent with them. This approach stimulates your brain, and gradually, whenever you encounter reminders or others mention the loss, your brain automatically recalls the joyful memories shared with your beloved.

Consistent practice is the key to achieving this transformation, often referred to as brain rewiring. Our brain's functioning is heavily influenced by its programming. Over the years, we have deeply ingrained the association of our beloved ones with happiness into our minds. Consequently, when they are no longer around, these memories trigger feelings of sadness. Reprogramming the brain is a challenging task due to the years of reinforcement behind these associations. Nevertheless, Neuro-linguistic Programming (NLP) offers valuable assistance in accelerating the journey back to a state of normalcy within a shorter timeframe.

Supporting someone who is grieving:

When a family member, friend, or colleague experiences the loss of a loved one, it is essential to be mindful of certain etiquette. In this guide, we will outline the dos and don'ts of providing support to help them navigate through their grief.

Do’s:

• Encourage them to speak and express their feelings openly. Alternatively, if they prefer to be quiet, offer support by merely being a comforting presence.

• Your presence can provide immense strength and comfort to the grieving individual.

Don'ts:

• When visiting someone who is experiencing loss and pain, refrain from discussing unrelated topics or sharing stories about someone else's similar experiences. Doing so might unintentionally convey the message that their pain is insignificant compared to others'.

Do's:

• Establish a comfortable and reassuring environment for them. Encourage their participation in meals and social activities.

• Provide hugs and assure them of your unwavering support during these difficult times.

Don'ts:

• Avoid placing blame on them or making them feel responsible for the loss. Each of us makes choices based on what we believe is best at the time. Even if mistakes were made, dwelling on them or assigning blame serves no purpose. It only adds to the person's grief and guilt, which they are already experiencing. Instead, focus on providing understanding and empathy during this difficult period.

Do's:

• Support and guide the person through the stages of grief, from denial to acceptance, by helping them recognize that grief is a natural part of life and offering spiritual perspectives if appropriate.

• Assist them in implementing coping mechanisms and techniques to navigate through their grief.

Don'ts:

• Refrain from telling the person to forget everything and move on abruptly, as it can exacerbate their situation. It is not realistic to expect them to stop grieving immediately. • Respect each person's individual way of expressing grief. Some may cry and shout, while others may withdraw into silence. Avoid pressuring them to conform to societal expectations or asking them not to cry. Allow them the space to express their emotions in their own way.

Acknowledge that death is not the end. While finding immediate happiness after losing someone may not be feasible, understanding the aforementioned perspective can help lessen the duration of their suffering.

Death is just a comma in the sentence of LIFE.

Being cheerful

I have a vivid memory from my childhood when I thought of giving my mother a birthday gift. I was just 11 years old at the time, and I excitedly asked her, "Amma, your birthday is coming soon. Please tell me what you want." Holding my school books in hand, I eagerly awaited her answer. To my surprise, she replied, "You study well. When the world looks up to you, I feel immensely proud. That will be the best gift for me."

As I grew older and completed my degree, my father emphasized the importance of hard work. He believed that securing a government job would lead to a stable life, providing him with peace of mind. Time passed, and my grandmother would often ask about my marriage, expressing her desire to witness my happiness in wedlock. I couldn't help but wonder why they seemed to be postponing their own happiness, waiting for specific events to occur.

These instances left a lasting impression on me, underscoring our tendency to frequently postpone happiness, linking it to specific future milestones or accomplishments.

After a few years, when Kukki, my daughter, came into my life, there was a specific day when she was crawling and attempting to communicate with me. In that moment, my mind wandered, contemplating when she would start walking and speaking fluently. I imagined how wonderful it would be when she began attending school, providing me with some much-needed free time. Thoughts of her excelling in her studies and securing a good job filled my mind, bringing a sense of relief and peace about her future. I found myself getting caught up in an endless stream of thoughts, each projecting a future moment of happiness and tranquility. As a parent, I couldn't contain my joy, envisioning a future where my worries would diminish. It was during this moment that I became aware of the cyclical nature of these thoughts.

We all believe v strongly in the statements like

I will be happy if..................

Write down your version of

I will be happy if

1. ____

2. ____

3. ____

4. ____

5. ____

6. ____

7. ____

8. ____

9. ____

10. ____

Think back to the last time you experienced a genuine smile from the depths of your being, where your presence felt soulful, and your mind was free from questioning, exuding a sense of tranquility. Some of you may have encountered this during meditation classes. How much time do we usually spend meditating? Five minutes, twenty minutes, or perhaps we push ourselves to find half an hour amidst our busy schedules. If you have ever participated in such a program, you might have encountered something truly magical. The effects of meditation extend beyond the practice itself; they permeate throughout the day. The calmness cultivated in your subconscious mind creates space for greater productivity and unleashes your creative potential, surpassing the outcomes of a non-meditative day.

But what is the fundamental rationale behind the seemingly simple act of sitting quietly and witnessing such profound changes? During meditation, we bring conscious awareness to our breath while intentionally closing unnecessary mental tabs that often send pop-up notifications in the form of thoughts. We are guided not to give attention to these distractions and instead focus solely on our breath. Gradually, we establish a connection with the state of nothingness, where we may feel as if we are floating. We dwell in this state for a while and then return to our normal state.

In simple terms, meditation is all about being consciously present, fully aware of what we are doing. While random thoughts may arise, being conscious and mindful helps elevate our energy field, leading other background programs to automatically shut down. Meditation acts as a powerful antivirus, safeguarding and enhancing our overall well-being.

Now that you grasp the power of this incredible built-in tool we possess, imagine being able to tap into it for just 20 minutes and feeling fantastic, enabling you to work efficiently. Envision living in a continuous state of meditation, a state of consciousness where you are in perfect alignment with your higher self and one with nothingness at all times. The results will be truly astonishing.

In this state, you will truly be able to live and savor every moment of life. You might argue, "But Akshata, I am already living and happy. I enjoy parties and outings." While that may be true, have you noticed that your happiness is often dependent on external factors? It could be a person, a situation, or a possession. This kind of happiness is not genuine; it's merely fleeting pleasure. It's like enjoying a piece of candy - it provides a temporary burst of joy. However, if your happiness relies on a specific person in your life, what happens if that person turns out to be unpleasant or leaves this world? If your happiness is tied to your current position, your car, your house, or your vacation, remember that all these things are temporary. Once you attain what you desire, you may soon yearn for something even greater. In essence, if you hand over the key to your happiness to your desires, you will never experience true happiness because nothing in this world is permanent, and our desires are constantly changing.

If I wait for my baby to start walking to find happiness, I overlook the precious moments of watching my baby crawl. If I believe I will only be happy after securing a job, I neglect the freedom I currently have to go anywhere without seeking permission from a boss, without attending meetings or answering phone calls. If I think I will be happy only after getting married, I fail to appreciate the joy of being with myself, savoring a cup of coffee with my favorite book as my sole company. This is a completely different kind of pleasure. And the secret is, until you can find contentment and happiness within yourself, the universe will not grant you a lifelong partner.

Every element in this world possesses its own unique beauty. We haven't come into existence solely to engage in cleaning, cooking, working for sustenance, and reproducing. These activities are part of a continuous process that has no definitive end, except for the moment when we take our final breath. Therefore, it is crucial to cherish every moment of our lives and be grateful for the gift of oxygen that sustains us.

Expressing gratitude to the universe, the ultimate supreme power, allows us to discover that all the answers and solutions reside within ourselves. By learning to value our own creation, we unlock the potential to find fulfillment and contentment.

Being joyful and feeling it within even without any reason will be our real victory for life.

Chapter 14
Practical Meditation:

Although we have already discussed meditation and its remarkable powers, in this chapter, we will explore its practical application. By following the steps outlined here, you will truly embrace the universe and, in essence, "DISCOVER THE UNIVERSE WITHIN YOU."

Find a comfortable position, close your eyes, and gently focus on your breath. As you do so, you will notice a plethora of thoughts emerging in your mind. This is because our minds are constantly active, filled with considerations such as what to cook for breakfast, how to complete assignments, or whether to take a break. Let these thoughts come and go without trying to suppress them, while maintaining your focus on your breath.

Keep in mind that it is a universal rule that nothing lasts forever, including our unwanted thoughts. If you stop giving them importance, they will naturally diminish. After a while, you will begin to sense the rhythm of your breath and your heartbeat. Now, imagine yourself expanding beyond your physical body. Visualize that you are not just occupying your own space but also merging with the chair you are sitting on, becoming one with the fan, and extending your presence to include the trees. Envision yourself within the entirety of your family, encompassing your father, mother, and spouse. Extend this perception to include your children as well. How does this panoramic view appear? Picture yourself rising from your seated position, with all the trees, clouds, furniture, siblings, spouse, parents, colleagues, and mountains taking that same step with you.

Continue your ascent, rising slowly until you see the whole expanse above the clouds, gradually reaching outer space. From this vantage point, observe planet Earth. Visualize that you are Earth, encompassing the oceans, the lush greenery, and everything that inhabits it. Now, ascend even higher and become the other planets in our solar system—Jupiter, Pluto, Mercury, and all the others. Extend your consciousness further until you become the entire Milky Way galaxy. Observe the countless planets and galaxies that exist as an extension of yourself. Align yourself within this vast cosmic network and take one step at a time, sensing the universe moving in sync with your every movement. Bend slightly, and you will notice the universe bending in unison. What a magnificent and awe-inspiring sensation this is!

Experience the enchantment, the divine power within you. As you merge with the universe, begin to return gradually, releasing one element at a time. Let go of your connection with the planets, then Earth. Observe yourself above the sky, then release your ties to your country, state, hometown, and neighborhood. Detach from your dwelling and various objects like the fan and chair. Now, you are left with your physical body, and if you detach even from that, you embody pure consciousness—the inner light that remains with you. Gently rub your palms together, bring warmth to your eyes, and slowly open them.

INNER GLOW & COSMIC BLISS
EXPERIENCE THE UNIVERSE WITHIN

This is more than just meditation; it is a pathway to connect with the divine. Take a moment to contemplate the following questions:

If everything in the universe is an extension of you, with whom are you angry?

Whom do you fear?

Do you genuinely desire to triumph over others?

What is causing your distress? Why do you shed tears for those who have passed away?

The answer to everything is this: When everything and everyone is a part of me, there is no need to fear anything. If I become angry with someone, I am essentially directing anger towards a part of myself. When someone achieves victory, it is also a triumph for me. If someone is facing difficulties, it becomes a challenge for me as well. Therefore, helping others is a way of helping ourselves. Why should we shed tears over someone who has left us when everything is interconnected, and that person is also a part of us?

In my belief, meditation is not something that requires a dedicated time and space to practice. Instead, it should be integrated into our daily lives and can be done anytime and anywhere. And how can you do it? It's quite simple!

Whenever you encounter challenges, simply affirm to yourself:

- I am energy.
- I am the source. I have everything I need and lack nothing.
- Regardless of the circumstances around me, I navigate with ease.

- Everything I desire resides within me. (Feel your breath.)
- I am protected, loved, and guided by the universe.
- My life unfolds in perfect synchronicity.
- The universe supports me unconditionally.
- The universe has grand plans for me.
- I trust the divine timing of my life.
- I am open to new opportunities.
- I live in alignment with my authentic self.
- I welcome the light of the universe into my life.
- I am connected to the loving presence of the mighty universe.
- I am one with the power of the universe.
- I am the universe, and the universe is within me.

Post face

I believe it is essential to recap all that we have learned together, as it allows us to connect with a better version of ourselves. By now, you might have noticed some positive changes within you, radiating positivity to those around you. If that is the case, I kindly request you to share that positivity with at least one person you encounter each day.

Unlike other motivational and life-changing books, I have aimed to keep things simple to reach a wider audience. As you have experienced, this book is not a one-way street; it is more of a conversation with yourself and your consciousness. If you have already read, practiced, and wholeheartedly engaged in the activities and exercises provided in this book, you now possess a comprehensive guide offering effective solutions to all the challenges you have faced in life.

This lays the foundation for life skills that are not typically taught to you. Yes, I emphasize "skills" because the teachings compiled here are not about providing immediate answers to your problems. Instead, my goal is for my readers to learn how to navigate through life's challenges more effectively. You may have the thought that you have already read the book, Akshata, and yet you still have ongoing issues. I agree, we encounter challenges throughout our lives, but how we face them matters. Even a monk has their own challenges, but they navigate through them much more swiftly than an average person. That's because a monk, and all those successful individuals like Ratan Tata, M.S. Dhoni, A.P.J. Abdul Kalam, Swami Vivekananda, Dr. B.R.

Ambedkar, and many others, focus on developing their LIFE SKILLS rather than solely seeking solutions to fleeting problems.

Most of our problems are like bubbles, and even if we don't actively address them, they will eventually disappear. So, let's shift our focus towards adopting the teachings in this book as life skills by:

- Tuning our frequency to attract our goals.
- Monitoring our actions throughout the day and responding to situations instead of reacting.
- Embracing books as friends rather than welcoming negative vibrations.
- Having an ultimate life vision.
- Aligning our needs with our goals. Remember, contributing to the universe is the highest form of prayer one can ever perform. How can we do that? By helping others in any possible way we can. We can bring happiness to people's lives through singing, dancing, or performing if we are artists, or by providing education to at least one underprivileged child if we are involved in teaching. We can treat animals with care and love. When we approach everything with utmost gratitude, self-awareness, and love in our hearts, I guarantee you that you will never suffer from any of life's issues because this world, this universe, is made by the Almighty and is indeed a beautiful place to live in.

Love your work more than money. It's essential to understand that money is a byproduct, an exchange of energy for the work we do in the office. It's simple: if you focus solely on money while working, you will indeed receive it as a result of your efforts. It's the law of attraction. However, if you genuinely love the work, put in your efforts, and find joy in the process while helping others overcome their problems, imagine the unconditional love, blessings, and abundance that will flow to you. The more selflessly we invest in raising the frequencies in others' lives, the more our own prosperity increases exponentially.

Let's not forget that we are all interconnected at the energy level, and all the energy we send to others reflects back to us. So, let's send good thoughts, blessings, appreciations, and positivity to receive the same in abundance.

Until next time...

Keep spreading love...